DELEUZE AND PSYCHOANALYSIS
PHILOSOPHICAL ESSAYS ON DELEUZE'S DEBATE WITH PSYCHOANALYSIS

FIGURES OF THE UNCONSCIOUS 9

Editorial Board   PHILIPPE VAN HAUTE
                  (Radboud University Nijmegen, the Netherlands)
                  PAUL MOYAERT
                  (Catholic University of Leuven, Belgium)
                  JOS CORVELEYN
                  (Catholic University Leuven, Belgium)
                  MONIQUE DAVID-MÉNARD
                  (Université Paris VII – Diderot, France)
                  VLADIMIR SAFATLE
                  (University of São Paulo, Brazil)
                  CHARLES SHEPHERDSON
                  (State University of New York at Albany, USA)

Advisory Board   TOMAS GEYSKENS
                  (Leuven, Belgium)
                  ELISSA MARDER
                  (Emory University, Atlanta, USA)
                  CELINE SURPRENANT
                  (University of Sussex, United Kingdom)
                  JEAN FLORENCE
                  (Université Catholique de Louvain, Belgium)
                  PATRICK GUYOMARD
                  (Université Paris VII – Diderot, France)
                  ELIZABETH ROTTENBERG
                  (De Paul University, Chicago, USA)
                  JEFF BLOECHL
                  (Boston College, USA)
                  PATRICK VANDERMEERSCH
                  (University of Groningen, the Netherlands)
                  VERONICA VASTERLING
                  (Radboud University Nijmegen, the Netherlands)
                  HERMAN WESTERINK
                  (University of Vienna, Austria)
                  WILFRIED VER EECKE
                  (Georgetown University, USA)
                  RUDOLF BERNET
                  (Catholic University Leuven, Belgium)
                  ARI HIRVONEN
                  (University of Helsinki, Finland)
                  JOHAN VAN DER WALT
                  (University of Glasgow, United Kingdom)
                  STELLA SANDFORD
                  (Middlesex University, United Kingdom)
                  CLAUDIO OLIVEIRA
                  (Federal University of Rio de Janeiro, Brazil)

DELEUZE AND PSYCHOANALYSIS

Philosophical Essays on Deleuze's Debate
with Psychoanalysis

Edited by Leen De Bolle

LEUVEN UNIVERSITY PRESS

© 2010 by Leuven University Press / Universitaire Pers Leuven / Presses Universitaires de Louvain. Minderbroedersstraat 4, B-3000 Leuven (Belgium)

All rights reserved. Except in those cases expressly determined by law, no part of this publication may be multiplied, saved in an automated datafile or made public in any way whatsoever without the express prior written consent of the publishers.

ISBN 978 90 5867 796 9
D/ 2010 / 1869 / 4
NUR: 777

Cover illustration: Juan Uslé, Pa-ti-pan, 2004-2005 (vinyl, dispersion and pigments on canvas, 31x46 cm, Private collection, Brussels; Courtesy Tim Van Laere Gallery, Antwerp)
Cover design: Griet Van Haute
Lay-out: Friedemann BVBA

Table of Contents

Preface: Desire and Schizophrenia Leen De Bolle	7
You Can't Have it Both Ways: Deleuze or Lacan Peter Hallward	33
Desire and the Dialectics of Love: Deleuze, Canguilhem, and the Philosophy of Desire Christian Kerslake	51
Anti-Oedipus: The Work of Resistance Lyat Friedman	83
Literature as Symptomatology: Gilles Deleuze on Sacher-Masoch Tomas Geyskens	103
Deleuze with Masoch Éric Alliez	117
Deleuze's Passive Syntheses of Time and the Dissolved Self Leen De Bolle	131
Epilogue Leen De Bolle	157
List of Contributors	159

Preface: Desire and Schizophrenia

Leen De Bolle

Gilles Deleuze is well-known as a philosopher who has profoundly and extensively debated with psychoanalysis. These discussions are situated in the aftermath of the revolutionary climate of May '68. In spite of his detailed and far reaching debates with psychoanalytical theory, Deleuze can hardly be reduced to a critic of psychoanalysis alone. The universe in which he thinks and writes is chaotic, divergent, heterogeneous, and plural. It is a universe consisting of a variety of concepts, authors, ideas, and traditions. Not only philosophy, but also many other disciplines, are present throughout Deleuze's oeuvre: literature, poetry, mathematics, physics, biology, theatre, dance, architecture, and so on. All of these disciplines have their own points of view or different perspectives. Instead of being opposed to each other or finding themselves in contradiction to one another, however, all of these disciplines contribute to the rich patchwork of Deleuze's rhizomatic style. The rhizome is a subterranean root that branches off into many directions without a beginning or an end. The different disciplines, authors, or systems make up the many different entrances or exits of the rhizome.

Nevertheless, Deleuze is—like Henri Bergson—convinced of the fact that an important author always thinks through one and the same idea. A great author formulates an idea and remains loyal to it, exploring and refining this idea through his entire oeuvre. This could also be said of Deleuze. In spite of the divergent directions of his thinking, the rhizomatic pluralism, the many references to a variety of disciplines and authors, the nervous and extremely dense style of writing, he remains loyal to one and the same intuition. Not only his early works, but also the later ones, are impregnated with the same idea: philosophy needs to be liberated from the systems or those moments that restrain it: the one, the truth, the good, the object, the subject, God, or man. Deleuze's philosophy is always situated in the sphere of free and unbound thinking that is released from the burden of representation, of the primacy of the *cogito*, of intentional consciousness, of phenomenology, of pathology, of the Oedipus-complex, and so on. This all fits very well with what Deleuze calls his 'nomad philosophy.' The nomad is the one, *par excellence*, who is freed from a fixed place, a fixed identity. During his travels, the nomad has to create his identity over and over again. The nomad breaks out of the given orders, the institutional settings, and so forth. He carries his roots on his back. He has no origin, no native country.

This absolute liberation can easily be associated with the revolutionary context of May '68. One can hardly deny that Deleuze was a product of his time, but as is the case with all great thinkers, his original style of thinking and his profound discussions with all kinds of authors in the history of philosophy show that his work transgresses the boundaries of the historical context. His discussions with psychoanalysis should be seen in the wider context of a great thinker who has invented his own style of writing, his own vocabulary, and his own philosophical system.

It is true that psychoanalysis became the companion, the rival, and the intimate enemy of Deleuze's philosophy. But times have changed, and nowadays it is interesting to see what we can still learn from these earlier discussions. This volume consists of various contributions that shed new or different lights on them. Each contribution is a different point of view or a different entrance into the 'rhizomatic' thinking of Deleuze. But let us, first of all, by way of introduction, have a closer look at the fundamental issues that are at stake in the debate between Deleuze and psychoanalysis.

To the negative sphere of psychoanalysis, the pathological figures, traumas, sad youths, repressions, projections, compulsive behaviours, and unfulfilled desires, Deleuze opposes the creative and productive forces of the unconscious. Instead of *representing* the unconscious, he finds it much more interesting to explore the wild and uncontrolled productions of the unconscious without repressing them. In his early works, he shows a great deal of interest in all sorts of authors or artists who do justice to the creative forces of the unconscious: Bergson, Nietzsche, Leibniz, Artaud, Bacon, Beckett, and Proust. Many concepts that are mentioned both in the theories of Deleuze and in psychoanalysis, such as repetition, remembrance, desire, pleasure, death instinct, perversion, schizophrenia, and so on, are used by Deleuze in the context of a vitalist philosophy that accentuates the production of the new. In this vitalism, he always stresses the positivity of desire, of the unconscious, of being. Following Bergson, Deleuze rejects negativity as a problem that originates from representational thinking. According to Bergson, negativity refers to a negative judgment. Initially, he states, we experience reality in its full plenitude, in the complete affirmation of all that is, and to which, secondarily, the negative judgment is added. The negative judgment is the negation of a judgment that is originally positive (Bergson 1941, 286). Deleuze is also inspired by the Nietzschean idea of affirmation. He agrees with Nietzsche that the greatest powers of life are instinctive, elementary forces that are original and authentic. All negative and reactive forces should be eliminated in favour of a pure affirmation of life.

Deleuze's discussions with psychoanalytical authors are always affected by these vitalist assumptions. Insofar as psychoanalytical ideas do not agree with them, Deleuze will call them in question. His relation to psychoanalytical theory, however, is more complicated than merely one of opposition. To say that Deleuze is *opposed to* psychoanalysis is already intrinsically problematic. His critique of representational thinking does not allow notions such as 'opposition,' 'contradiction,' 'negation,' and so on. Consequently, it would be unjust to state that Deleuze opposes himself to psychoanalysis for the sake of opposition, as would be the case in a dialectical strategy. Nowadays, opinions about Deleuze's relation to psychoanalysis are mixed. Deleuze's own attitude towards it evolved over the years, from more or less sympathetic to more or less hostile. But in any case, the basic assumptions of psychoanalytical metapsychology do not easily reconcile with Deleuze's vitalist ideas. The question is, then: why did Deleuze debate so often with psychoanalysis, if it was not for the sake of opposition? The answer has to do with the specific themes that are treated by both psychoanalysis and Deleuze. A theory of desire, of the unconscious, of repetition, of the dissolution of the ego, is at stake. These are all the concepts that make up parts of Deleuze's philosophy of 'a life.' Whereas Freud and his successors tried to discipline the forces of the unconscious, to enfeeble them, and to put them out of action, Deleuze, on the contrary, stresses the rich, creative, and even artistic forces of a productive unconscious. This suggests that his fundamental critiques of psychoanalysis are the necessary conditions for the development of his own theories of desire, of repetition, of the unconscious.

In regard to the problematic notion of 'opposition,' it is interesting to mention the proper style of Deleuze's philosophy, the specific method that he developed and that he elucidates in *Dialogues*, the method of 'pick-me-up' or 'pick-up': "in the dictionary = collecting up, chance, restarting of the motor, getting onto the wavelength" (Deleuze 1977, 8). Instead of arguing with psychoanalysis by means of logical argumentation, for the sake of being right, he picks up what is of interest to him and moves on. Instead of discussion, or polemic, philosophy thereby becomes a series of coordinations. Rather than saying 'Deleuze against Freud' or 'Deleuze against Kant' or 'Deleuze against Lacan,' we should say 'Deleuze and Freud' ... and Kant ... and Lacan. In *Dialogues*, Deleuze says that "the conjunction AND" is not "a union, nor a juxtaposition, but the birth of a stammering, the outline of a broken line which always sets off at right angles, a sort of active and creative line of flight?

AND... AND... AND..." (Deleuze 1977, 7–8). These lines of flight must enable the thinker to get past a problem. For Deleuze, it does not matter that much to find a solution to a problem, but rather to find a line of flight, to get past a problem and to go on ... In his approach to the great thinkers of the history of philosophy and other authors, he is more interested in the creative outcome of the encounter between those theories and his own assumptions, rather than in opposing himself to them or elaborating their diverging views. Deleuze never gives the impression of wasting time on endless discussions for the sake of being right. He replaces the dominant notion of 'truth' in classical philosophy with the notion of creativity. What matters is not that something would be true or false, but rather whether something is strong enough to be productive. In his philosophical method, Deleuze really functions as a philosophy-machine. This philosophy-machine continuously produces thought as the result of an encounter with various systems, authors, streams of thought, or styles of thinking. This means that Deleuze's theories of desire are also the product of an encounter with, among other things, psychoanalysis. But whereas he indeed 'picks-up' some basic ideas from psychoanalysis in the early works, he gradually finds out that it cannot ultimately be reconciled with his own thoughts.

In the early works *Difference and Repetition* and *The Logic of Sense*, Freud, Klein, Lacan, Ferenczi, Jung, and Laplanche appear in the context of Deleuze's critique of 'the image of thought' that consists in representational thinking. In *Difference and Repetition*, Freud in particular is sometimes mentioned as a welcome companion who is of great use to Deleuze, in order to clarify his own theories of repetition. Some other times Deleuze finds himself strongly opposed to Freud's theories of death drive, desire, repetition, and so forth. Already in the introduction of the book, Deleuze discusses Freud's conception of repetition.

Freud and repetition

Generally speaking, Deleuze does not agree with the idea that repetition would be a reaction formation that appears as a result of a failure of remembrance or recognition, as Freud claimed in his earlier work. According to these earlier writings, repetition is inversely proportional to remembrance. The less one can remember a representation under the condition of resistance, the more one will repeat oneself. Repetition then, has a compulsive character. It has no meaning in itself. It is not an original, autonomous movement, but appears to be a mechanism of reaction or of defence.

For Deleuze, however, repetition itself has a fully positive meaning. It is an original force that coincides with life itself and that acts independently of any representational thinking. It is not a response to a failure of remembrance or a desperate way to deal with it, or a way to get cured, just as remembrance itself would not be a cure. Deleuze states: "We are not therefore, healed by simple anamnesis, any more then we are made ill by amnesia [...]. If repetition makes us ill, it also heals us; if it unchains and destroys us, it also frees us ..." (Deleuze 1968a, 19). Repetition is the proper movement of what he calls 'the problematic.' The problematic is the positive texture of life. It consists of the continuation of problems and questions that produce a variety of figures and forms. The problematic is a notion that Deleuze does not reserve for cognitive or conscious acts alone. It does not disappear when a solution is found to a problem. Following the fundamental ontological theories of Heidegger, Deleuze conceives of the problematic as an aspect of being itself, which constantly poses its problems and questions. The problematic concerns all the great questions of life and death, love and hate, pleasure and pain, sexual differences, and so on. According to Deleuze, these are questions that can not be reduced to oppositional representations or dualisms. They cannot be represented by logical propositions or dialectical structures. The problematic consists of all the differences, the embryonic or germinative elements, the intentions of desire and unconscious wishes that install themselves in between the two terms of an opposition. Instead of the clear and distinct positions of oppositional terms, the problematic is populated by a variety of unconscious forces and constellations. It produces a phantasmagoria of figures and forms that replaces the dualist representations and never refers to an ultimate solution or representation. Deleuze states:

> There are no ultimate or original responses or solutions, there are only problem-questions, in the guise of a mask behind every mask and a displacement behind every place. It would be naïve to think that the problems of life and death, love and the difference between the sexes are amenable to their scientific solutions and positings ... (Deleuze 1968a, 107)

After having criticised the concept of repetition as a reaction to repression in Freud's earlier texts, Deleuze, strangely enough, seems to appreciate the fact that Freud discovered in his later work, namely in the text 'Beyond the Pleasure Principle,' a positive reason for repetition that is termed the 'death drive.' This drive generates a repetition that intends to return, a repetition that is essentially conservative. As a result of his observation of the repetitive game of a little child and of the phenomenon of traumatic neurosis in soldiers returning from the front, he discovers a repetition that is not governed by the pleasure principle: the death drive. Freud goes on to consider this death drive as a cosmological principle that governs all living creatures. This is a great revolution in Freud's thinking. Whereas before, he considered the destructive drives as being submitted to the pleasure principle or the reality principle, the death drive now acquires a completely different meaning. Repetition becomes an original movement that is no longer related to the psychological experiences of the empirical.

Deleuze, however, does not fully agree with Freud in respect to this death drive. He appreciates the fact that the death drive works independently of any empirical principle and becomes a positive reason for repetition, but he disagrees with the fact that, for Freud, the death drive figures in a materialistic model. Repetition as death drive tends to return to a stage before life, to a stage of death as unanimated matter. In this context, life in its biological sense is opposed to death. As such, Freud never abandons the idea of a dualistic model, consisting of conflicting forces and antagonistic principles. Whereas Freud opposed ego to lust, or reality to pleasure, before 'Beyond the Pleasure Principle,' since then he substitutes this dualism with the opposition between life and death; Deleuze, on the contrary, wants to free desire from any dualistic model. Desire is not a force of conflict or contradiction. The unconscious, for Deleuze, is not dualistic but problematical, serial, iterative … This is also the reason why Deleuze prefers the notion of 'death instinct' to that of 'death drive.' The death instinct, as he understands it, stands for the impersonal energy of 'a life' that transcends the conflicts of a particular life.

Rather than the great oppositional representations of Freud, Deleuze prefers the differential texture of a Leibnizian unconscious. In this kind of differential unconscious, the great oppositional representations are substituted with a multitude of small perceptions. These small perceptions are unconscious, virtual, embryonic elements that tend to form a global perception that can reach the threshold of consciousness. Normally, when we are awake, in the daylight of conscious life, we are not aware of these small perceptions, but when a person falls asleep, the small perceptions start to move. Leibniz compares sleep, in this sense, with death. Inspired by this theory, Deleuze refers to the death instinct as an interesting condition that opens up a rich domain of thousands of small perceptions. This assumption testifies to a strong belief in the original power of a death instinct. Inspired by Blanchot, Deleuze conceives of death not as the end of mortal life, but as the source of the problematic. Death is not…

the limitation imposed by matter upon mortal life, nor the opposition between matter and immortal life, which furnishes death with its prototype. Death is, rather, the last form of the problematic, the source of all problems and questions, the sign of their persistence over and above every response, the 'Where?' and 'When?' which designate this (non)-being where every affirmation is nourished ... (Deleuze 1968a, 112)

As such, death has two distinct aspects: 1.) the disappearance of the person, the reduction to zero of this difference that constitutes the ego; 2.) a state of free floating differences that are no longer submitted to the form of the ego or the person. The first aspect is personal. It concerns the death of the person. It is the death that can be confronted by the ego in a struggle or in an experience through which everything passes. The second aspect has no relation to the ego. It is an impersonal death that is "always coming, the source of an incessant multiple adventure in a persistent question" (Deleuze 1968a, 112).

Deleuze criticises Freud for only having considered the first aspect. Following Blanchot, he elaborates the second aspect as the essential dynamics of desire. The death instinct then stands for a complete liberation of energy from the objects and from the form of the ego (i.e. the libidinal energy is withdrawn from the objects and undergoes a process of desexualisation). This dissolved energy, however, does not return to inanimate matter, but instead constitutes an immanent plane of desire through which the energy endlessly circulates. This is an immanent plane that is no longer bound to the ego; it happens outside of the ego. As such, the death instinct forms a radical 'outside' (*dehors*). It is something to which there is no possible relation, something that we cannot control or discipline. We are surrendered to it in such a way that we lose all willpower. But nevertheless, according to Blanchot and Deleuze, this radical 'outside' that is not opposed to life or pleasure needs to be affirmed. It can be compared to the inspiration of the artist or the poet. Inspiration is, like death, a radical outside that cannot be controlled by a subject but that nevertheless has to be affirmed. Deleuze states that Freud has failed to understand the full implications of 'death instinct' because he never considered such a (spiritual) conception of death.

In spite of these discussions with Freud in *Difference and Repetition*, Deleuze 'picks-up' a great deal of psychoanalytical theory. In regard to Lacan and Klein, he is mainly fairly positive in these early works, especially in *The Logic of Sense*. But, even as Deleuze tries to connect with the theories of Freud, Klein, and others, such that he sympathizes more or less with them, it is nonetheless clear in these early books that he already creates the conditions for the ruthless attacks on psychoanalyses in his later works: the volumes *Capitalism and Schizophrenia* (*Anti-Oedipus* and *A Thousand Plateaus*) and his *Dialogues* with Claire Parnet. In these books, in which he does not hide his distaste for psychoanalysis any longer, Deleuze develops an effective collaboration with the psychoanalyst Félix Guattari. Together, they create their own theory of desire, in debate and discussion with psychoanalysis. Whereas Freud and others appear in Deleuze's earlier works mostly in the context of his critique of representation, of his renewal of 'the image of thought' and the ontological or metaphysical systems that they imply, Deleuze and Guattari address themselves, in their *Capitalism and Schizophrenia*, directly to psychoanalytical theory for the sake of a theory of desire itself. It is in these volumes that we find the most controversial, the most extreme statements concerning desire and schizophrenia. The discussion with psychoanalytical theory takes here, at times, a very hostile character.

In these volumes, Deleuze and Guattari confront the idea that desire is imprisoned by the domestic figures of the Oedipal triangle or that it is a lack of being. They strongly affirm the reality of an unlimited desire, a desire that lacks nothing. The idea that desire lacks nothing follows from Deleuze's Spinozist background.

Spinoza and desire

Three years before *Anti-Oedipus*, Deleuze published his book *Spinoza and the Problem of Expression*, in which he meticulously comments on Spinoza's philosophy of immanence and his theory of the affects, as presented in particular in the *Ethics*. Through his entire oeuvre, Deleuze remains loyal to his Spinozist inspirations. Next to Bergson and Nietzsche, Spinoza is the third big player in Deleuze's vitalism. In *Difference and Repetition*, Spinoza is significant in the context of his metaphysical and ontological theories. But his influence is not restricted to theoretical questions alone. The Spinozist notion of desire plays an important role in Deleuze's work. It is omnipresent between the lines of *Capitalism and Schizophrenia*. The main idea in this respect is that, for Spinoza, desire lacks nothing. It lacks nothing because it is not defined by the tendency towards an object. Whereas Freud interprets desire mainly as a state of need that can be fulfilled by its proper object, or through a hallucinatory satisfaction, it is, for Spinoza, the positive essence of every being. When Freud discusses the loss of the object as a result of a withdrawal of libidinal energy from the object (i.e. desexualisation), this can lead to all kinds of pathological syndromes. For Spinoza, on the contrary, there is no object from the beginning. Desire, or what he calls *conatus*, is the tendency by which "each thing, insofar as it is in itself, endeavours to persevere in its being" (Spinoza 1677, III.6). To this proposition he adds: "The effort by which each thing endeavours to persevere in its own being is nothing but the actual essence of the thing itself" (Spinoza 1677, III.7). Spinoza also explains that when this tendency only concerns the mind, it is called *will*, but when it concerns mind and body, it is called *appetitus*. If one is self-conscious of this *appetitus*, Spinoza speaks of *desire*. Desire is the *conatus* that has become self-conscious. Spinoza concludes:

> For what has been said, it is plain, therefore, that we neither strive for, wish, seek, nor desire anything because we think it to be good, but on the contrary, we adjudge a thing to be good because we strive for, wish, seek or desire it. (Spinoza 1677, III.9)

Desire is a force that acts independently of objects, as a pure striving that constitutes the essence of a thing. The *conatus* constitutes a certain capacity (i.e. power) to be affected. The gradation by which a thing can be affected by exterior things without being destroyed in this confrontation is the power or the capacity of that thing. Consequently, the *conatus* can also be defined as the tendency to keep open the capacity to be affected to the greatest degree. Deleuze stresses the fact that the *conatus* must not be understood as the tendency to move over from non-existence to existence (Deleuze 1968b, 230). He emphasises that, for Spinoza, the *conatus* is characterized by no lack whatsoever. The *conatus* is at every moment what it can be. It is the continuation and affirmation of the being of a thing. There is no exterior goal, no object for desire to aim at. Desire consists in the preservation of itself in the complete, positive presence of what it can.

This Spinozist background of Deleuze's explains why he strongly rejects the idea that desire would refer to an ontological lack, a lack of being. Deleuze also rejects every idea that imprisons desire in conflict or reaction mechanism. In *Anti-Oedipus*, Deleuze and Guattari criticize all those theories that send desire off to the office of the psychiatrist or that hide it behind the curtains of the theatre. They claim that desire should not be repressed, denied, or hidden. Deleuze and Guattari notice that Freud and his disciples indeed discovered the domain of desire as a bundle of free floating streams of energy, namely the Id, but that later on they shrunk back from the wild and explosive excesses of it. They also mention the fact that it was a big mistake for Freud to use the definite article, saying 'the' Id (Deleuze & Guattari 1972, 1). According to Deleuze and Guattari, Freud tried to control the forces of the unconscious by imposing an order on it. They reproach him for having represented unconscious desires via the image of the theatre, more precisely through the order of the classical Greek theatre.

Oedipus versus the desiring machines

In the story of Oedipus, Freud discovers an analogy with desire in the familial situation. With the figure of Oedipus, the stream of desire becomes connected with objects or persons like the father or the mother. At the same time, desire is repressed behind the curtains of the theatre, where it becomes enfeebled and disempowered. The Oedipal triangle has the meaning and the significance of an institution of desire. It takes place within the triangle that represents a determinate order: father-mother-child. The child stops where the mother begins, the mother stops where the father begins. Everyone has to stick to his or her place. But the problem, Deleuze and Guattari notice, is that psychoanalysis has never precisely determined where exactly each person begins and who is who (e.g. the child identifies with the father, it addresses its pleasure to the mother ...).

According to Deleuze and Guattari, the unconscious should be affirmed in its plenitude as an unlimited production of desire. Desire cannot be put on stage; it is a factory, an atelier, a workplace. They consider the image of the factory far more appropriate than the image of the theatre for the unlimited and impersonal flows of desire. The great variety of fantastic images and hallucinations that it produces are not reaction formations or defence mechanisms that result from unconscious conflicts or oppositions. As Bergson already pointed out (and Deleuze and Guattari fully agree), fantasies and hallucinations have a completely positive meaning, since they add something new to reality instead of testifying to a lack. As long as fantasies are bound to the figures of the ego, the person, the mother, or the father, they remain restricted to a negative meaning. Consequently, Deleuze and Guattari state that the unconscious does not know any persons; it has no family. The unconscious is an orphan. The discovery of the auto-production of desire coincides with the discovery of the Cartesian *cogito* that it is also without parents.

To the three poles of the Oedipal triangle, Deleuze and Guattari propose a multitude of desiring machines: "it is at work everywhere, functioning smoothly at times, at other times in fits and starts. It breathes, it heats, it eats. It shits and fucks ... Everywhere *it* is machines" (Deleuze & Guattari 1972, 1). There are only machines and machines of machines that dispose of an autonomous activity without there being a moment, divine or human, a social community or culture that regulates or controls them.

The notion of 'machine' needs to be distinguished from the notion of 'mechanism.' A mechanism is a closed system in which an imposed movement progresses by means of hinges, wires, springs, and so on. A mechanism fits in a determinist worldview. It works by means of determinate causal relations. The operations that it realises are predictable and can be anticipated. A machine, on the contrary, forms an open system, which means that it is productive and creative. Its productions are not determined beforehand, nor are they the result of a determinate order. They do not correspond to fixed causal relations or to a prototype or model. Rather, they are heterogeneous and plural.

By conceiving of desire as a desiring machine, Deleuze and Guattari draw attention to the uncontrolled productivity of desire. Desire is a stream, a stream or a wave into which flow all kinds of connections, junctions, and circuits, as, for instance, between the body and an organ. In this respect, one could say that the mother's breast is a source machine that is connected to an organic machine: the mouth of the child. Partial objects (e.g. the mouth, the breast, the anus …) that are connected by streams (e.g. the milking machine) do not represent the mother or the father. They are parts of the desiring machine that refer to processes which are irreducible to the Oedipal triangle. A playing child explores the house: "it contemplates an electric plug, it uses its body as a machine: a leg becomes an oar … it manipulates its little cars …" (Deleuze & Guattari 1972, 55). Deleuze and Guattari notice that the presence of the parents is indeed continuous and that the child cannot live without the caring and loving presence of his parents, but they say that this is not the question at stake. The question is rather what the place and the function of the mother and the father is in this world of partial objects. The question is whether everything that is touched or discovered by the child refers to the mother or the father. The answer to this question is negative:

> Ever since birth, his crib, his mother's breast, her nipple, his bowel movements are desiring-machines connected to parts of his body. It seems to us self-contradictory to maintain, on the one hand, that the child lives among partial objects, and that on the other hand he conceives of these partial objects as being his parents, or even different parts of his parents' bodies. Strictly speaking, it is not true that a baby experiences his mother's breast as a separate part of her body. It exists rather, as a part of a desiring-machine connected to the baby's mouth, and is experienced as an object providing a non-personal flow of milk, be it copious or scanty. (Deleuze & Guattari 1972, 47)

In this sense, desire is continuously (re)produced. Desire is not something that comes from the mother, nor does it come from the child; it is not subjective or intersubjective. The partial objects and the streams of desire represent nothing. They are the condition for a distribution of roles and actors, but they are not of the nature of persons or of the subjective in general. The reverse is rather the case; the subject is a product of the desiring machine. It originates in the connections and junctions of the machines. The subject as a product of the machine is always a residue that exists next to the machine. It is a subject without identity that continuously comes into being with every connection. By revealing this anti-Oedipal nature of desire, Deleuze and Guattari want to draw attention to its real nature. This nature, however, cannot be conceived by means of an *a priori* conception. It is not the question 'what is desire?' that is at stake, but rather the question 'does it function?' and 'how does it function?'

The desiring machine connects, absorbs, and consumes the free floating energy. As such, it respects the dynamic and mouldable character of libidinal energy. The connections and consumptions of these flows of energy do not stop the machine; they are, on the contrary, its conditions for productivity. They are not the object of an analysis, but rather a synthesis of desire that produces new subdivisions with each connection. The consumption is not a destruction of energy; it is a passage, a transit, or a crossing over.

The functioning of the desiring machine leaves no place whatsoever for any form of deficiency or lack. It produces the real in its plenitude. For Freud, on the contrary, the infantile fantasy exists in contradiction with reality. Since his basic assumption consists in the Oedipal triangle, he consequently has to conceive of social and metaphysical relations as something that comes afterwards, as something that cannot directly be invested by desire. For Deleuze and Guattari, however, the machines of social, technical, or metaphysical production are similar to the desiring machine. The production of desire coincides with the other productions. The libidinal energy invests in a social world. It flows through groups, populations, tribes. Unlike the psychoanalytical assumption, desire thus does not create a kind of compensation. It is not limited to a particular mode of existence, but it is rather productive in all kinds of material and social productions. As such, the desiring machine does not create the imaginary, nor the symbolic, but the real. Anne Sauvagnargues states:

> The machine takes the place of the models of the symbolic structure or the imaginary fantasy, it rejects the structural models, the formal stylistics that are inspired by linguistics and by psychoanalytical interpretation. [...] It substitutes the interpretation by a principle of

experimentation and of connection that is directly political and not imaginary, private or individual, not ideal and formally symbolic. [...] the machine retakes the function of the symbolic signifier of Lacan and produces the subject as a residue of its functioning, but this production should be conceived, like Marx did, as historical and social and not signifying and private. (Sauvagnargues 2005, 133)

The machines produce the real without lack. Like the *conatus* of Spinoza, they have no object. The only object of the machine is the machine itself. The only thing that the machine misses from the viewpoint of representational thinking is that which restricts its productivity: a subject with a fixed identity. If there is the production of a subject, then it is a subject that wanders around the machine as a residue, as a nomadic subject.

The idea of a dissolution or a splitting of the subject that characterizes the nomadic subject— and that Deleuze has already discussed in the context of his critique of representation in *Difference and Repetition* and *Logic of Sense*— acquires now, in the volumes of *Capitalism and Schizophrenia*, the name of a 'schizophrenic' machine. With their concept of schizophrenia, Deleuze and Guattari descry the model *par excellence* for the liberation of desire.

Schizophrenia

The term 'schizophrenia' was originally coined by Bleuer (1911) to designate a cluster of psychoses which Kraeplin had demonstrated more or less fall under the same category (Laplanche & Pontalis 1967, 433). The name that was given by Kraeplin was dementia praecox. The common characteristic of these psychoses consisted in a fundamental symptom: splitting [Spaltung]. Clinically speaking, the following characteristics are usually attributed to schizophrenia: incoherence of speech, incoherence of acting, and incoherence of affect, dissociation with reality, withdrawal into oneself, the predominance of an interior life in which one is dedicated to the production of fantasies, an insane activity that is more or less explicit and that is chaotic and unstructured.

Usually, two moments in schizophrenia are distinguished. The first moment consists in the breakdown of bonds with reality. The schizophrenic extracts all libidinal energy from the surrounding objects, and thus all energy flows back to the ego. The result of this process of desexualisation is a general feeling of detachment from reality. The second moment consists in the delusion, the hallucination.

At first, the schizophrenic loses all contact with reality. The world is gone and its normal organisations, meanings, contents, and objectives are lost. The most well-known example of it is the case of Schreber, which has been commented upon by both Freud and Deleuze and Guattari. Daniel Paul Schreber suffered from an extreme form of paranoia [*dementia paranoides*]. His case history consisted of three periods of illness with intervening periods of normal functioning. The research into the Schreber case could rely on detailed descriptions of his hallucinations, because Schreber himself had described and published the history of his illness under the title *Denkwürdigkeiten eines Nervenkranken* (1903).

In respect to the loss of reality, Freud remarks that "he (Schreber) could not bring himself to doubt that during his illness the world had come to an end and that, in spite of everything, the one that he now saw before him was a different one" (SE 12, 69). The delusion that accompanies this loss of reality is interpreted by Freud as an attempt at restitution, an attempt to reconstruct a (new) world: "And the paranoiac builds it again, not more splendid, it is true, but at least so that he can once more live in it. He builds it up by the work of his delusion. *The delusional formation, which we take to be the pathological product, is in reality an attempt at recovery, a process of reconstruction*" (SE 12, 71).

Freud claims that the libidinal energy flows back to the ego as a consequence of the withdrawal of energy from objects. This dissolution of energy alone, however, is not enough to result in paranoia. The dissolved energy can result in various outcomes that are not destructive (i.e. it is also the condition for the processes of idealisation and sublimation). In normal life, the libido is constantly withdrawn from objects without resulting in sickness. According to Freud, the additional factor that provokes paranoia has to do with all kinds of failures in the process of repression. Interior perceptions that have to remain repressed find themselves fixated in a particular stage of the development of the drive. In the case of paranoia, the energy flows back to the ego and brings about a fixation in narcissism.

In the case of Schreber, Freud relates the failed repression to repressed homosexual inclinations. Schreber suffers from a *"fixation at that stage of narcissism* owing to *the step back from sublimated homosexuality to narcissism* which is a measure of the amount of *regression* characteristic of paranoia." (SE 12, 72) Subsequently, he deduces that these homosexual inclinations stem from a repressed father complex which came from his childhood. Schreber's hallucinations are therefore said to result from his disturbed relationship with his father. In this scenario, his delusions about God refer in the first place to his doctor in the psychiatric hospital, Doctor Flechsig, which, in turn, refers to Schreber's father. The most fantastic hallucinations and delusions are said to be the result of a combination of a dissolved libido and a father complex.

In *Anti-Oedipus* however, Deleuze and Guattari present a totally different interpretation. They agree with Freud that paranoia is indeed characterised by a dissolution of libidinal energy, what they would call disjunctive energy: a mobile, mouldable energy, always ready to be transformed and displaced. What they object to in Freud is that he relates this dissolved energy to the figure of the father. This is a way of wrongly maintaining the Oedipal triangle, because the psychotic products burst from all sides out of the too-simple figure of it. According to Deleuze and Guattari, delusions and hallucinations are the products of a desiring machine. Instead of being imprisoned in himself, Schreber produces various effects of desire. He "feels something, produces something, and is capable of explaining the process theoretically" (Deleuze & Guattari 1972, 2). Deleuze and Guattari state that the schizophrenic is in direct contact with the deepest and most invisible forces of life that have dissolved all fixed forms and symbols into intensive, molecular, germinative flows or cosmic elements. Schreber is capable of connecting these flows, disconnecting them, consuming, producing, or reproducing them. A 'divine, cosmic energy' flows through Schreber's body. He has the delusion of all kinds of rays of light tracking through his body: a solar energy. Deleuze and Guattari do not interpret this as a metaphor as Freud did, for whom the sun was a symbol of the father. They consider it the effective product of desire. *The delusion is, for Deleuze and Guattari, not an attempt at restitution, but rather a reterritorialisation of desire.* The dissolved energy becomes reterritorialised into a multitude of heterogeneous, intensive, molecular, and cosmic elements. The hallucinations are creations of desire. They are not illusive. Deleuze and Guattari state that the products of desire are productions of the real. Its effects are really lived through. Therefore, the schizophrenic is not characterized by a loss of reality. Instead of a loss of reality, Deleuze and Guattari claim that the schizophrenic finds himself closer to the beating heart of reality: "Far from having lost who knows what contact with life, the schizophrenic is closest to the beating heart of reality, to an intense point identical with the production of the real, and that leads Reich to say: 'What belongs specifically to the schizophrenic patient is that ... he experiences the vital biology of the body...'" (Deleuze & Guattari 1972, 96).

When the libidinal energy withdraws from objects and becomes desexualised, it does not lead to a detachment from reality but, on the contrary, to an unlimited production and creation of various realities. Deleuze and Guattari's theory of desire thus has ontological implications. Their conception of reality is not the one with which we are familiar since childhood, the reality that we know through various processes of socialisation and that assigns to each thing its fixed place by means of a symbolic order, to which one has to correspond and in which one finds his or her own place. Reality, therefore, is not a pre-given order that one can enter into as an adult after having overcome the infantile fantasies. On the contrary, Deleuze and Guattari present 'an image of thought' that stands for a multitude of realities or points of view that are never acquired once and for all, but that have to be created in every new contact with life. Schizophrenia is interesting in this respect because it is the figure *par excellence* that produces 'an image of thinking' that does not depart from a pre-given order. The schizophrenic finds himself outside of every symbolic order that is oriented towards the 'name of the father.' To obtain this liberation of desire, Deleuze and Guattari deem it necessary to liberate schizophrenia from the forms of autism, psychiatric hospitals, or a disconnection from reality. The dissolved energy then becomes a free floating, mobile energy, capable of continuous transformation and displacement. Against illness, Deleuze and Guattari oppose a radical and indestructible belief in life.

Their conception of schizophrenia is, however, difficult to accept. It is not easy to understand how Deleuze and Guattari reconcile their conception with a strong and powerful belief in life. After all, schizophrenia concerns a dissociation of the person, a disintegration of the mind and even of the body. One could say that Deleuze and Guattari use the notion of schizophrenia in a metaphorical way, or as an analogy to clarify the new 'image of thought' that they oppose to the old image of thought, the thinking of representation. But this is absolutely not the case. They warn several times against conceiving their newly created concepts in terms of metaphors. They repeatedly stress the fact that we should take their concepts literally. The rejection of this metaphorical way of interpreting their concepts is justified from the standpoint of their conception of schizophrenia itself: schizophrenics themselves are characterized by a process of disintegration that affects the use of language, and this is called de-metaphorisation.

De-metaphorisation

This process of de-metaphorisation, which is described by Freud as a symptom of illness, is, strangely enough, celebrated by Deleuze and Guattari as the process par excellence of their theory of desire. In The Unconscious, Freud investigates how language can be disturbed in the initial phase of schizophrenia:

> In schizophrenics we observe—especially in the initial stages, which are so instructive—a number of changes in speech [...]. The patient often devotes peculiar care to his way of expressing himself, which becomes 'stilted' and 'precious.' The construction of his sentences undergoes a peculiar disorganization, making them so incomprehensible to us that his remarks seem nonsensical. Some reference to bodily organs or innervations is often given prominence in the content of these remarks (SE 14, 197)

As an example, Freud mentions the case of a girl who was brought to hospital after a quarrel with her boyfriend. She finds herself in the initial phase of schizophrenia and complains that:

> *her eyes were not right, they were twisted.* This she herself explained by bringing forward a series of reproaches against her lover in coherent language. 'She could not understand him at all, he looks different every time, he was a hypocrite, an eye-twister, he had twisted her eyes, now she had twisted eyes; they were not her eyes any more; now she saw the world with different eyes.' (SE 14, 198)

The figure of speech in German '*jemandem die Augen (den Kopf) verdrehen,*' has also the metaphorical meaning of 'deceiver.' In this case, the girl takes the metaphor literally. This is what Freud calls hypochondriac language or organ speech (SE 14, 198). It is a consequence of de-metaphorisation. The mechanism that underlies the process of de-metaphorisation is situated between the pre-conscious and conscious systems. In order to pass through consciousness, the unconscious representations have to pass along the transitory system of the pre-conscious that disposes of word-representations and word-associations. These word-representations are connected to thing-representations that are in line with the unconscious traces of memory. In the case of schizophrenia, the libido is completely withdrawn from objects, a process that is accompanied by a loss of reality. The disconnection of the libido, however, can be so extreme that it is also withdrawn from the memory-images of objects. The schizophrenic has severed the bonds not only with reality but also with the entire content of his or her personal history. As a result of de-metaphorisation, there is a loss of the thing-representations (i.e. they are not repressed but are rather lost forever) and the word-representations play freely. The verbal expressions lose all connection to things and are experienced as direct, physical affections. Hence the notion of 'organ-language.'

Whereas metaphorical expressions refer to an exterior framework of the symbolic for the healthy person, they cause a fundamental disintegration of the bodily condition of the schizophrenic. The schizophrenic falls apart. Nevertheless, it is this highly problematic process, and the disintegration of the body that accompanies it, that Deleuze and Guattari interpret as a positive aspect of their philosophy of becoming. In *The Logic of Sense*, Deleuze does not deny the cruel and painful aspects of schizophrenia, but he also maintains that these cruel forces should be affirmed. As a result of various examples from literature (e.g. Lewis Carroll and Artaud), Deleuze develops, in line with the processes of de-metaphorisation and inspired by Spinoza, a language of the body: "A pure language-affect is substituted for the effect of language" (Deleuze 1969, 88). The schizophrenic no longer circulates at the surface of clear and distinct forms and figures; he dives into the shapeless and obscure depths of the body. At these depths, there are no more clear distinctions between words and things. In this respect, Deleuze talks about the body as a sieve:

> The first schizophrenic evidence is that the surface has split open. Things and propositions have no longer any frontier between them, precisely because bodies have no surface. The primary aspect of the schizophrenic body is that it is a sort of body-sieve. (Deleuze 1969, 86–87)

With this idea of the body-sieve, Deleuze is conforming to the Spinozist formula: 'No one has thus far stipulated what a body can do.' The phrase 'what a body can do' refers, for Spinoza, to the capacity of a body to be affected by other bodies without being destroyed by them. Especially in the process of de-metaphorisation, the body is continuously affected by other bodies in more or less violent ways. Deleuze states: "Everything is a mixture of bodies and inside the body, interlocking and penetration… Other bodies always penetrate our body and coexist with its parts" (Deleuze 1969, 87).

As previously mentioned, Deleuze does not deny the cruelty of the forces of de-metaphorisation. He asserts that words are projectiles that enter the body in a most painful way. The word "loses its sense, it bursts into pieces; it is decomposed into syllables, letters and above all, into consonants which act directly on the body, penetrating and bruising it" (Deleuze 1969, 87). In spite of this cruel disintegration of the body, however, he finds it unnecessary to return to the normal order of things. Instead of a restoration of the normal order and a repression of the forces and powers of the body, the key is to use them for new ways of feeling and thinking:

> For the schizophrenic, then, it is less a question of recovering meaning than of destroying the word, of conjuring up the affect, and of transforming the painful passion of the body into a triumphant action,

obedience into command, always in this depth beneath the fissured surface. (Deleuze 1969, 88)

The violence of a language in which words become projectiles must be transformed into a language that consists of breaths, cries, and sighs. This kind of language corresponds to a "glorious body ... being a new dimension of the schizophrenic body, an organism without parts, which operates entirely by insufflation, respiration, evaporation, and fluid transmission" (Deleuze 1969, 88). The language of the schizophrenic allows literature and art to discover new worlds underneath the clear surface of the distinct forms; it opens up an obscure depth of forces that enter into communication without mediation.

The schizophrenic body and language, however, are not only relevant in an artistic context, although they find their expression *par excellence* in these domains. In the first place, Deleuze argues that his schizo-analysis, at its core, has a profound philosophical meaning. Throughout his entire oeuvre, he stresses the fact that all of his concepts have to be taken literally and not metaphorically. This fits into a complicated ontological framework, in a theory of being. The ontological implications of the schizo-analysis are expressed in the well-known concept of 'body without organs,' to which Deleuze and Guattari dedicate a whole chapter in their *A Thousand Plateaus*.

The body without organs

Following Artaud, Deleuze and Guattari refer to the schizophrenic body as a body without organs. It is a body in an advanced state of decomposition. Artaud uses this notion to demonstrate how the body in the theatre is penetrated by affects. It consists of holes and pieces, comparable with the infection of the body by the plague. In the body without organs, the streams of energy are no longer bound to the specific functions of the different organs, but instead find their way through a body without organs. In this respect, Artaud presents a theatre of cruelty. Dark forces triumph, as in the case of great myths that talk about the first bloodshed, the division of the sexes, torture and slaughter. But in spite of this violence and cruelty, Artaud defends a fundamental affirmation of all the forces of life. Theatre must enable us to liberate all repressed desires. We must believe in the renewal of life by theatre. Therefore, it is necessary, Artaud tells us, to 'break' language in order to be able to touch life. He affirms life in all its aspects, even its darkness and cruelty. Theatre "unravels conflicts, it releases powers, it puts possibilities in motion and if these possibilities are dark, then the plague or theatre should not be blamed, but life itself" (Artaud

1968a, 45; my translation). He declares war on the organs: the organs, or rather the organism, is the enemy of the body. The organism imposes an order on it, restricting the capacities of the affected body. As such, the body is no longer a functioning unity of which desire is only an aspect, but, on the contrary, it coincides completely with desire. There is one great body of desire.

Deleuze and Guattari state that this body is infinite. It is not restricted by subjects or objects, by one's proper name or personal history, nor limited by the demands of reality or the symbolic order. The body without organs is everything, and outside of it, there is nothing, or rather: it is—like the death instinct that Deleuze discussed in *Difference and Repetition*—the outside of desire. As such, desire finds itself no longer in relation to an exterior instance that is opposed to the body without organs, but instead it circulates over the infinite surface of a body whose holes are passages, bridges, or tunnels. The decomposition of the body does not refer to a destruction of the body but rather to different intensive zones and layers of it. The body without organs is an immanent plane of desire: "The BwO is the field of immanence of desire, the plane of consistency specific to desire (with desire defined as a process of production without reference to any exterior agency, whether it be a lack that hollows it out or a pleasure that fills it.)" (Deleuze & Guattari 1980, 170–171). When there is no lack and no satisfaction, desire can continue to circulate endlessly. Deleuze and Guattari mention two examples in this respect: courtly love and masochism. (Notice that they use those two phenomena in one and the same breath.) The objective of the masochist is not pain or humiliation. This is only the price he pays for postponing the experience of satisfaction. As a result, desire in its full positivity can be extended to infinity. It fills itself by itself; it is immanent and thus infinite. Also, in courtly love, desire is not oriented towards a transcendent ideal or the overcoming of a lack, nor is it the abandonment of desire in favour of a higher objective. What is at stake, on the contrary, is that desire finds itself in a situation in which there is no lack whatsoever, in which it is fulfilled by itself. Pleasure then coincides with desire. In courtly love, everything is admitted, except those things that would restrict desire: satisfaction or any transcendent instance that subordinates desire to an exterior instance. Every such instance would impose an organism on the body without organs, and the organism is, as Artaud said, the enemy of the body. Instead, the uncontrolled growth of desire should be affirmed. This is the consequence of a vitalist intuition that is connected to pleasure but also to pain, to beauty but also to cruelty. The body without organs is a cancer that infects and deforms everything. This appears literally to be the case for Schreber. He is literally a body without organs that is constantly affected and infected by desire. In one of his delusions, he is convinced of the fact that he has already passed away and experiences his body in an advanced state of decomposition. His organs are affected by processes of decay: "He lived for a long time without a stomach, without intestines, almost without lungs, with a torn oesophagus, without a bladder, and with shattered ribs ..." (Deleuze & Guattari 1983, 9; quoting Freud).

According to Deleuze and Guattari, however, not only psychotics like Schreber, but all of us, must construct a body without organs. In this respect, they claim that the body without organs is a practice, not a theory or a concept. In *A Thousand Plateaus*, they express themselves dramatically: "Find your body without organs. Find out how to make it. It's a question of life and death, youth and old age, sadness and joy. It is where everything is played out" (Deleuze & Guattari 1980, 167). And they add: "Where psychoanalysis says, 'Stop, find yourself again,' we should say instead, 'Let's go further still, we haven't found our BwO yet, we haven't sufficiently dismantled our self'" (Deleuze & Guattari 1980, 167). Apparently, they show little or no consideration for the diseased aspects of schizophrenia:

> Is it really so sad and dangerous to be fed up with seeing with your eyes, breathing with your lungs, swallowing with your mouth, talking with your tongue, thinking with your brain, having an anus and larynx, head and legs? Why not walk on your head, sing with your sinuses, see through your skin, breath with your belly ... (Deleuze & Guattari 1980, 167)

In *Capitalism and Schizophrenia*, Deleuze and Guattari engage a ruthless and uncompromising battle against psychoanalysis, a battle that is inspired by their radically vitalist intuition. Against the objection that this is an unjust glorification of madness, Deleuze argues that he does not glorify madness for the sake of madness, but that he tries to extract 'life' out of it. In *Dialogues*, he states:

> I hear the objection: with your puny sympathy you make use of lunatics, you sing the praises of madness, then you drop them, you only go so far ... This is not true. We are trying to extract from love all possession, all identification to become capable of loving. We are trying to extract from madness the life which it contains, while hating the lunatics who constantly kill life, turn it against itself. (Deleuze 1977, 40)

Nevertheless, their radical affirmation of the schizophrenic body is difficult to accept. They affirm, very strongly, the creative power of disintegration and decomposition. This suggests that Deleuze and Guattari present a philosophical theory of desire with far-reaching ontological assumptions, rather than offering an alternative to psychoanalytical treatment. Their concept of schizophrenia opens our minds to new ways of thinking and feeling. It opens up the arts and literature to new works and challenges. To the dogmatic order of symbolic mediation with which we are acquainted by means of processes of socialisation, they oppose the creation of different worlds, different realities that are all the expressions of one desire. Desire expresses itself in the same sense in many different constellations. The underlying ontological implications of this 'univocal' expression bring us back to Deleuze's Spinozist inspirations.

Spinoza and the schizophrenic

Deleuze and Guattari identify the body without organs with the *Ethics* of Spinoza:

> After all, is not Spinoza's *Ethics*, the great book of the BwO? The attributes are types or genuses of BwO's, substances, powers, zero intensities as matrices of production. The modes are everything that comes to pass: waves and vibrations, migrations, thresholds and gradients, intensities produced in a given type of substance starting from a given matrix. (Deleuze & Guattari 1980, 170)

As such, the body without organs has a metaphysical meaning. Desire thus exceeds every mental or psychic dimension, becoming being itself. It becomes, like being for Spinoza, an infinite substance that is present in each of its expressions. This is the consequence of a radical de-metaphorisation. The body without organs is no metaphor. Desire is not *like* a body without organs, it *is* the body without organs and the body without organs *is*. It is being itself, which proceeds to the expression of the real without any mediation. The desiring machine jumps from threshold to threshold, from intensity to intensity, across its immanent surface.

In *A Thousand Plateaus*, Deleuze and Guattari state: "Drug users, masochists, schizophrenics, lovers—all BwO's pay homage to Spinoza" (Deleuze & Guattari 1980, 170). This means that they do not conceive of Spinoza's philosophy as a theoretical and abstract metaphysics, but interpret it, on the contrary, as a philosophy that is not concerned with knowledge, but rather experience. Deleuze stresses that Spinoza always thinks in terms of feeling and experiencing: "We feel and we experience. He [Spinoza] does not say: we think [...] we feel and we experience that we are eternal" (Deleuze 1981, 1).

When Deleuze and Guattari identify the body without organs with the *Ethics* of Spinoza, they have in mind in particular the third book about the affects. It is in this book that the definition of the *conatus* appears. According to Spinoza's definition, the *conatus* stands for the capacity to be affected; as such, it is the essence of each thing. When this capacity is transgressed, the body decomposes and dies. This decomposition, however, must not be understood as deficiency, as a failing or weakness, but rather as the extreme point of the capacity to be affected. In the case of Schreber, one could say that he had an extraordinary capacity to be affected. His body endured the most extreme mutilations, but was never completely destroyed by delusion. He died of natural causes that came to him after gradual decay, in spring 1911. Whereas Freud thought that delusion is an attempt at restoration by means of finding the way back to the symbolic order, Deleuze states, following Spinoza, that everything is real. Delusion does not exist in a relationship of analogy or resemblance with reality; it is the direct expression of the real. Deleuze continuously mentions that Spinoza rejects every symbolic dimension. The symbolic, to him, is only a confused idea of the imagination. Deleuze explains that Spinoza is not in line with the tradition of Adam and the prophets, the tradition of men obeying God as legislator. When God forbids Adam to eat the apple, Adam wrongly interprets this command as an interdiction that expresses the will of God. Consequently, the prophets have always searched for 'signs' as the symbolic confirmation of the law of God. To Spinoza, however, God has only tried to explain something to Adam, namely the fact that the apple would poison him. This poison is not merely a metaphor or a symbol but rather a physical reality. If there is an order for Spinoza, then it is the order of nature.

Against the idea that delusion has a curative function that recovers contact with the symbolic, Deleuze stipulates that delusion cures as well as sickens. In one of his hallucinations, Schreber is, for instance, convinced of the fact that he has already passed away and that his organs have started to decompose, but, he survives this mutilation because his delusion of decay is accompanied by a religious delusion in which he imagines that all kinds of divine rays pass through his body:

> He lived for a long time without a stomach, without intestines, almost without lungs, with a torn oesophagus, without a bladder, and with shattered ribs, he used sometimes to swallow part of his own larynx with his food, etc. But divine miracles ('rays') always restored what had been destroyed. (SE 12, 17)

Schreber's capacity to be affected is brought dangerously near its limit by delusion, but, at the same time, he is saved by delusion. The only thing that matters for Deleuze is the capacity of the body to be affected. Spinozism allows one to say the same about delusion as what Deleuze says about repetition, namely: "If repetition makes us ill, it also heals us; if it unchains and destroys us, it also frees us, testifying in both cases to its 'demonic' power" (Deleuze 1968a, 19).

With this statement, Deleuze expresses his radical vitalism. Sickness and health are immanent forces of life. This statement clarifies the conviction of Deleuze and Guattari that we should stop searching for all kinds of interpretations or models to explain delusion, but that instead we should dive into life itself to be cured or not cured ...

* * *

More then 35 years after the publication of *Anti-Oedipus*, the radical, uncompromising statements made by Deleuze and Guattari concerning desire and schizophrenia have led to an immense production of literature. Many commentators draw attention to the fact that Deleuze's oeuvre cannot be read without accepting the profound influence of the theories of Freud, Lacan, Klein, and so on. Others maintain that Deleuze's philosophy can under no circumstances be reconciled with psychoanalytical theory. But the time has come to go beyond the insults and misunderstandings that have characterized the debate between Deleuze and psychoanalysis up to this point. This does not mean that time has erased all differences. Rather, the contributions in this volume elucidate the philosophical implications of this 'Deleuze *and* psychoanalysis.'

In 'You Can't Have it Both Ways: Deleuze or Lacan,' Peter Hallward argues that, although the agreement between Deleuze and Lacan seems to go a long way, in the end their ideas on desire diverge fundamentally. This is not surprising since, as Christian Kerslake shows in his 'Desire and the Dialectics of Love,' Deleuze came from a very different tradition of thinking about desire. His ideas are not inspired by Freud, but from the beginning of the 1950s by Leibniz, Proust, Jung, and Spinoza. Therefore, the problem of love is much more central in Deleuze's philosophy than in psychoanalysis.

Rather than opposing the theories of Freud, Lacan, Deleuze, and Butler, Lyat Friedman's '"Anti-Oedipus": The Work of Resistance' presents these thinkers as moments in a strange history of resistance. Freud's shocking sexual interpretations, which dazzled his patients and himself, became 'interesting,' accepted, and expected. Therefore, Lacan, Deleuze, and Butler had to invent new interpretations that could be resisted by new analyses.

The papers of Tomas Geyskens and Éric Alliez focus on Deleuze's relation to Sacher-Masoch and masochism. They investigate Deleuze's ideas about the essential relation between the literary and the clinical as a way of disentangling the confusion between sadism and masochism, as it is found in psychoanalysis. Tomas Geyskens' 'Literature as Symptomatology' analyses the formal differences between Sade's and Masoch's writings. In this way, a more fundamental difference comes into view: while sadism is a rationalistic programme based on the destruction of the personal sphere and the promotion of a cold apathy produced by pure reason, masochism is the art of suspense and suggestion, aimed at a radical de-genitalisation of sexuality. In 'Deleuze with Masoch,' Éric Alliez elaborates on this connection between Deleuze and Masoch. Deleuze's critique of psychoanalysis is only the starting point for the creation of a 'Deleuzian politics.'

Leen De Bolle investigates Deleuze's paradoxical notion of a dissolved self as a result of three fundamental repetitions of the unconscious: the passive syntheses of time. These passive syntheses constitute a pre-individual transcendental field that is populated by unconscious contractions, contemplations, partial objects, virtual memories, desires, and dreams. Its transcendental conditions are situated in a pure event in which all disjunctive forces coexist: pleasure and pain, life and death, sickness and health. As such, the impersonal event can be affirmed, even when the subject has dissolved.

Bibliography

Artaud, A. 1968. *Le théâtre et son double*. Paris: Gallimard, 1968.
Bergson, H. 1941. *L'Evolution créatrice*. Paris: PUF, 2001.
Deleuze, G. 1968a. *Difference and Repetition*. Translated by P. Patton. London: Athlone, 1994.
———. 1968b. *Expressionism in Philosophy: Spinoza*. Translated by M. Joughin. New York: Zone Books, 1992.
———. 1969. *The Logic of Sense*. Translated by M. Lester and C. Stivale. Edited by C. V. Boundas. London: Athlone, 1990.
———. 1981. "Spinoza lesson at Vincennes, 17/03/1981." http://www.webdeleuze.com/php/texte.php?cle=43&groupe=Spinoza&langue=1
Deleuze, G., and C. Parnet. 1977. *Dialogues*. Translated by H. Tomlinson and B. Habberjam. London: Continuum, 2002.
Deleuze, G., and F. Guattari. 1972. *Anti-Oedipus: Capitalism and Schizophrenia*. Translated by R. Hurley, M. Seem, and H. R. Lane. Minneapolis: University of Minnesota Press, 1983.
———. 1980. *A Thousand Plateaus: Capitalism and Schizophrenia*. Translated by B. Massumi, London: Continuum, 2004.
Freud, S. 1911. "The Case of Schreber." SE 12.
———. 1915. "The Unconscious." SE 14.
———. 1920. "Beyond the Pleasure Principle." SE 18.

———. 1923. "The Ego and the Id." SE 19.
Laplanche, J., and J.-B. Pontalis. 1967. *Vocabulaire de la psychanalyse*. Paris: PUF, 2004.
Sauvagnargues, A. 2005. *Deleuze et l'art*. Paris: PUF, 2005.
Spinoza, B. de. 1677. *Ethica*. Translated by A. H. Stirling, Kent: Wordsworth Editions, 2001.

You Can't Have it Both Ways: Deleuze or Lacan

Peter Hallward

Deleuze's general hostility to psychoanalysis in general is well known; his relation to Lacan in particular seems more obscure.

Deleuze's *Logic of Sense* (1969) concludes with long and enthusiastic references to concepts adapted to some degree from Lacan: castration, lack, the sublimation of drives, the phallus, Oedipus itself. When in *Anti-Oedipus* (1972) these concepts are brusquely abandoned along with the surface-depth relation they served to mediate, Lacan continues to appear in a mainly sympathetic light.[1] In *Anti-Oedipus* Deleuze and Guattari credit Lacan with nothing less than the discovery of 'the real production of desire,' desire understood in terms of "the 'real inorganisation' of the molecular elements [...], pure positive multiplicities where everything is possible, without exclusiveness or negation." If Deleuze and Guattari's assault on psychoanalysis is here subsumed within a more general critique of Oedipus (i.e. the repression of desire by representation, transcendence, and the economy of lack, cemented by the mediation of the family, the capitalist division of labour, and the configuration of the state), Lacan continues to appear as more of an ally than an opponent. Lacan is the analyst who subverts the logic of Oedipal mediation from within. Lacan is the analyst who began the process of "schizophrenizing the analytic field, instead of oedipalizing the psychotic field."[2] Deleuze and Guattari are confident that their "Lacan does not enclose the unconscious in an Oedipal structure. He shows on the contrary that Oedipus is imaginary, nothing but an image, a myth" (Deleuze & Guattari 1972, 310). Lacan dares to approach the point that Freud could not face – he is prepared to lead "Oedipus to the point of its self-critique," the point where structure "reveals its reverse side as a positive principle of nonconsistency which dissolves it" (311).

---

[1] In Gilles Deleuze's *Logic of Sense* (1969), "it is with Oedipus that the event is disengaged from its causes in depth, spreads itself at the surface and connects itself with its quasi-cause from the point of view of a dynamic genesis." It is thus largely thanks to Oedipus that psychoanalysis can still figure there as 'the science of events' and the 'art of counter-actualisations' (Deleuze1969, 211–212). Asked about *Logic of Sense* four years after it was published, Deleuze responded tersely: "I've undergone a change. The surface-depth opposition no longer concerns me" (Deleuze 2002, 261).

[2] Deleuze & Guattari 1972, 309–310; cf. 363.

This anti-Oedipal Lacan performs a number of other valuable services. He confirms the machinic nature of the unconscious (41). He traces the signifier to its true despotic origin, with 'vigour and serenity' (209). He rightly "assigns the cause of desire in a nonhuman 'object,' heterogeneous to the person, below the minimum conditions of identity, escaping the intersubjective co-ordinates as well as the world of meanings" (360).

The Lacan of *Anti-Oedipus*, in other words, is the psycho-analyst who most nearly becomes a schizo-analyst. Although *Anti-Oedipus* is already critical of many of Lacan's followers and readers, Lacan himself continues to figure as a valuable schizophrenic ally from within the psychoanalytic camp.

Over the course of the 1970s, however, Deleuze and Guattari's critique of psychoanalysis becomes increasingly radical and intransigent. By the mid 1970s, Deleuze tends to dismiss psychoanalysis en bloc as a sadistic apparatus that stifles the production of any genuine desire.[3] By the time he and Guattari publish *A Thousand Plateaus* (1980), nothing remains of their alliance with Lacan. Whenever psychoanalysis is discussed in this second volume of *Capitalism and Schizophrenia* it is subject to a global condemnation that appears to include Lacan along with his followers.[4] Prominent in *Anti-Oedipus*, Lacan is virtually absent in *A Thousand Plateaus*. He is directly mentioned only a couple of times, and in unambiguously critical terms: he is condemned, along with Freud, Brunswick, and Leclaire, for subjecting the Wolf-Man to interminable analysis (Deleuze & Guattari 1980, 26), and he is accused, along with Sartre, of maintaining an anthropomorphic, 'subjectivist' analysis of the gaze (171). By the time they come to write their fourth and final joint book, *What is Philosophy?*, Deleuze and Guattari do not so much as mention Lacan at all.

Does this evolution of Deleuze's relation to Lacan indicate a genuine ambivalence? Does it point to a significant shift in Deleuze's own philosophical priorities? Does it serve to open up a productive zone of theoretical overlap, a liminal zone of fertile synthesis and eclecticism? Or does it suggest, on the contrary, the gradual realisation of an essential divergence or incompatibility? In the brief notes that follow I will be defending this second alternative.

This divergence is not absolute, of course. Deleuze and Lacan both emphasise the primacy of differentiation and displacement, and they share a determination to dismantle the traditional, 'molar' or ego-centred subject. They share a contempt for the conscious, well-adapted subject of popular

---

[3] See, for instance, G. Deleuze, 'L'Interprétation des énoncés' [1977], in Deleuze 2003, 80ff.
[4] See, for example, Deleuze & Guattari 1980, 17–18, 34–35, 130–131, 151, 154–155, 259–260, 283–284, 288–289.

psychology. They share an aversion to the 'American way of life' and the *service des biens*, with all its associations. They pursue a comparably subtractive project of unbinding, *déliaison*, evacuation, disruption, defamiliarisation or de-territorialisation – the hollowing out of every form of imaginary solidity and depth, in favour of the austere intensity of desire or drive. They share, in short, a good many things.

Such shared concerns are certainly enough to set out a basis for comparison, but they still pale in significance with respect to a number of obvious and fundamental differences. These differences apply to Deleuze's and Guattari's conceptions of the subject, of the unconscious, of language and speech, of signification, of representation, of time, of the other, and so on. Considered in light of these differences, the appropriation of Lacan in *Anti-Oedipus* starts to seem selective and shallow, and difficult to reconcile with Deleuze and Guattari's own conception of desire and the unconscious. Considered along these lines, the eventual dismissal of Lacan in *A Thousand Plateaus* seems simply to make explicit the tension that underlay earlier attempts at appropriation.

Very schematically, the divergence between Deleuze and Lacan applies in at least five domains, all of which are likely to be thoroughly familiar to most readers of Lacan.

1. *The first and most substantial difference concerns the limits of the field of enquiry*

As I have tried to demonstrate elsewhere, Deleuze's main effort, after Bergson and Spinoza, is to develop ways of thinking and acting "that liberate man from the plane or level that is proper to him, in order to make him a creator, adequate to the whole movement of creation."[5] Deleuze's ontology equates being with creativity, or with inventive differentiation – being is creating, or to be is to differ.

Against the dialectical presumption that any given "thing differs with itself because it differs first with all that it is not," Deleuze everywhere affirms that a "thing differs with itself first, immediately," on account of the "internal explosive force" or differential creative power that animates it and makes it what it *is*.[6] There is no better description of Deleuze's general effort than Bergson's own affirmation of a cosmic creativity animated by an absolute or divine power of creating, so long as we remember that what matters is

---
[5] Deleuze 1966, 111.
[6] Deleuze, 'Bergson's Conception of Difference' [1956], in Deleuze 2002, 42.

always the active *creating* as such, rather than what is created – the *creans* (or *naturans*), rather than the *creaturum* (or *naturata*). "Everything is obscure in the idea of creation," Bergson reminds us, "if we think of *things* which are created and a *thing* which creates, as we habitually do. [... For] there *are* no things, there are only actions [...]. God thus defined has nothing of the already made; He is unceasing life, action, freedom. Creation, so conceived, is not a mystery; we experience it in ourselves when we act freely."[7]

If, then, forms of mysticism figure as the eventual telos for both Deleuze and Bergson's philosophy this is simply because "the ultimate end of mysticism is the establishment of a contact, consequently of a partial coincidence, with the creative effort which life itself manifests. This effort is of God, if it is not God himself. The great mystic is to be conceived as an individual being, capable of transcending the limitations imposed on the species by its material nature, thus continuing and extending the divine action."[8] The great mystics are people who become perfectly transparent vehicles for the singular creative force that surges through all living things. By leaping across all social and material boundaries, they achieve "identification of the human will with the divine will." They "simply open their souls to the oncoming wave" and become pure "instruments of God," such that "it is God who is acting through the soul in the soul."[9] The mystic (and to a lesser extent the artist, the dreamer, the philosopher ...) strives to become an adequate vehicle for creation *as such*—i.e. it is to participate in God's own "undertaking to create creators."[10]

If being is creating, then this implies: (i) that all existent things exist in one and the same way, univocally, as so many active creatings; (ii) that these (virtual) creatings are themselves aspects of a limitless and consequently singular creative power; (iii) that every creating gives rise to a derivative (actual) creature whose own power or creativity is limited by its material organisation, its situation, its capacities, its relations with other creatures, and so on; (iv) that the main task facing any such creature is to dissolve these limitations, in order to become a more immaculate vehicle for that virtual creating which alone individuates it. In the case of human creatures, this process involves first and foremost the dissolution of all those mental habits which sustain the illusion we have of ourselves as independent subjects preoccupied with the representation of other subjects or objects; it also involves the dissolution

---

[7] Bergson 1907, 248–249.
[8] Bergson 1932, 220–221. The mystic is that person to whom "creation will appear as God undertaking to create creators, that He may have, besides Himself, beings worthy of His love" (255).
[9] Bergson 1932, 229, 99, 232, 311.
[10] Bergson 1932, 234, 255.

of all the psychological, social, historical, territorial, and ultimately organic structures that enable these habits to continue. The decisive effort is always to break free of the determinate (social, organic, territorial ...) constraints that mediate our direct participation in reality – that immediate, overwhelming participation in reality which in *Anti-Oedipus* Deleuze and Guattari attribute to the figure of the schizophrenic, and which "brings the schizo as close as possible to the beating heart of reality [...], to an intense point identical with the production of the real."[11]

Hence the imperative to dissolve and 'deterritorialise' the organism, to follow a 'line of flight' that enables an 'absolute break' with the determinate limits of a situation.[12] Hence too the imperative to 'destratify' a situation: if creations proceed as continuous or 'molecular' lines of differentiation through a smooth 'plane of consistency,' created strata interrupt such lines. "Strata are what separate us from the plane of consistency [...], where there is no longer any regime of signs, where the line of flight effectuates its own potential positivity and deterritorialisation its absolute power. The problem, from this standpoint, is to tip the most favourable assemblage from its side facing the strata to its side facing the plane of consistency [...]. Destratify" (Deleuze & Guattari 1980, 134). And since "the principal strata binding human beings are the organism, significance and interpretation, and subjectification and subjection," so then our primary concern is "one of knowing how the individual would be able to transcend his form and his syntactical link with a world" in order to become the transparent vessel for that "non-organic life of things which burns us [...], which is the divine part in us, the spiritual relationship in which we are alone with God as light."[13] The general goal is to pursue a process of redemptive subtraction that is simultaneously an escape from all determined constraints and re-incorporation within the absolute determination of infinite creative power. Such redemption proceeds through the cultivation of "imperceptibility, indiscernibility, and impersonality—the three virtues. To reduce oneself to an abstract line, a trait, in order to find one's zone of indiscernibility with other traits, and in this way enter the haecceity and impersonality of the creator. One is then like grass: one has made the whole world into a becoming because one has suppressed in oneself everything that prevents us from slipping between things ..." (Deleuze & Guattari 1980, 279–280).

---

[11] Deleuze & Guattari 1972, 19, 87.
[12] See, in particular, Deleuze 1977, 38.
[13] Deleuze 1969, 178; Deleuze 1983, 54.

Deleuze's general effort, in short, assumes that the only distinctively human effort is to experiment with and invent appropriate means of becoming inhuman or extra-human. There can be no 'becoming-human' in Deleuze. To become is instead always to become extra-human: to become-animal, mineral, imperceptible ... "To move beyond the human condition, such is the meaning and direction [sens] of philosophy" (Deleuze 1986, 124–125).

Psychoanalysis, by contrast, retains in one form or another a constituent link with the specific constraints and circumstances of becoming-human. Even so anti-humanist a writer as Louis Althusser insists on this orientation in his 1964 essay on 'Freud and Lacan': the peculiar concern of psychoanalysis lies precisely in the quietly violent process whereby an infant grows up not as an animal, not as some sort of 'wolf-child' or 'ape-child,' but as a '*human child*.' Survival of this process is "the test all adult men have passed: they are the *never forgetful* witnesses, and very often the victims, of this victory, bearing in their most hidden, i.e. in their most clamorous parts, the wounds, weaknesses and stiffnesses that result from this struggle for human life or death." Psychoanalysis is concerned with this fundamental struggle, with

> the only war without memoirs or memorials, the war humanity pretends it has never declared, the war it always thinks it has won in advance, simply because humanity is nothing but surviving this war, living and bearing children as culture in human culture: a war which is continually declared in each of its sons, who, projected, deformed and rejected, are required, each by himself in solitude and against death, to take the long forced march which makes mammiferous larvae into human children, *masculine* or *feminine subjects*.[14]

For Deleuze, the 'human' denotes nothing more than a sort of local enclosure, an especially stubborn set of strata or territorial constraints. The human denotes the condition that any active or creative force must strive to escape, since "becoming-reactive is constitutive of man" (Deleuze 1962, 64): if an active force does what it is, and immediately creates, desires, or destroys, a reactive force introduces a gap between action and actor. Reactive force privileges the created over the creating. An active force creates or destroys; the bearer of a reactive force asks why it is being destroyed, resents its destroyer, and attributes malice to it. In the Nietzschean terms that Deleuze adopts and intensifies, "*ressentiment*, bad conscience and nihilism are not psychological traits but the foundation of the humanity in man. They are the principle of the human being as such" (Deleuze 1962, 64). The human being is simply

---

[14] Althusser 1964, 205–206.

that being which has taken on such resentment as its organising principle. An envious, belittling negativity or nihilism is constitutive of the human, and with the human "the whole world sinks and sickens, the whole of life is depreciated, everything known slides towards its own nothingness." Conversely, since humanity is indistinguishable from ressentiment, "to move beyond ressentiment is to attain the 'end of history as history of man'" (Deleuze 1962, 34–35). If truly creative life is to live it will require the death of man. Genuine affirmation will only proceed "above man, outside man, in the overman [*Übermensch*] which it produces and in the unknown that it brings with it" (Deleuze 1962, 177). To reverse in this way our creatural passage from 'the immediate to the useful' would allow us to go back to 'the dawn of our human experience.'[15] This dawn – the dawn of the world, of '*the world before man*, before our own dawn' – is a moment to which Deleuze will never cease to return.[16]

Lacan's work, by contrast, begins (with his 1932 thesis, *De la psychose paranoiaque dans ses rapports avec la personalité*) with an insistence on the irreducible need, in any analysis of human behaviour, of a social and semantic dimension, a dimension that cannot be subsumed within any more general science or metaphysics. Lacan's work begins with an analysis of how the emergence of human personality is mediated by the intersubjective work of interpretation and speech.

2. *This brings us to a second difference, concerning the status of subjectivity and intersubjectivity*

Lacan locates the 'object and method' of analysis 'in this specific reality of interpersonal relations.'[17] The peculiar concern, medium, and milieu of psychoanalysis is speech, and speech is by definition a trans-subjective activity. Speech is bound up in the need and struggle for recognition, the constitution of a subject in its relations with the other: "Language, prior to signifying something, signifies to someone."[18] Speech is a matter of seduction, dependence, deception, aggression, and so on, before it is a matter of information

---

[15] Bergson 1896, 185.
[16] Deleuze 1983, 68, 66; cf. 122, 81, Deleuze & Guattari 1980, 280; Deleuze 1993, 36–39.
[17] J. Lacan, 'Beyond the "Reality Principle,"' in Lacan 1966, 71.
[18] Ibid., 66. "This assumption by the subject of his history, insofar as it is constituted by speech addressed to another, is clearly the basis of the new method Freud called psychoanalysis" (J. Lacan, 'Function and Field of Speech and Language in Psychoanalysis,' in Lacan 1966, 213; cf. Lacan 1954, 264).

or description. Lacan's I is *I* because I speak to and with the Other, and 'my' unconscious is structured by the language that I share or contest with others – "the fact that the symbolic is located outside of man is the very notion of the unconscious."[19]

At the most general level, "what I seek in speech is the response of the other," and in this sense speech is always a pact, a form of symbolic being-with whose dynamic is most clearly exemplified by the logic of a *password*.[20] A password means nothing, other than the institution of a shared or socialised sphere of meaning itself – a sphere in which people can speak with (rather than assault) each other. For instance, if what is decisive in Lacan's analysis of Poe's 'Purloined Letter' is the way 'the signifier's displacement determines subjects' acts,' this signifier remains 'the symbol of a pact,' and its determination itself proceeds via the mediation of a stable and repetitive pattern of intersubjective relationships: what most interests Lacan "is the way in which the subjects, owing to their displacement, relay each other in the course of the intersubjective repetition."[21] What Lacan here calls the 'register of truth' is situated "at the very foundation of intersubjectivity. It is situated where the subject can grasp nothing but the very subjectivity that constitutes an Other as an absolute."[22]

Along with the intersubject, Deleuze rejects the category of the subject as well. As everyone knows, the subject in Lacan is the subject of unconscious speech, the subject defined by castration and lack, by its incorporation into a symbolic order that lacks any natural plenitude or positive orientation. There is no sub-symbolic or 'instinctual' order of things, no domain of being or nature, that can subsume the domain of the subject and speech. The subject of speech is both forever 'cut off from nature' and forever 'grafted' into his sociosymbolic milieu, the milieu in which 'desire is a relation of being to lack.'[23] The subject that constitutes itself (through the 'mirror stage') in its reflected disjunction with itself 'consists' only in this lack of coincidence.[24]

In Deleuze, by contrast, operators of displacement or differentiation do not proceed in terms of negation and lack but in terms of continuous creation and dynamic metamorphosis. The Deleuzian 'subject' (the schizo, the nomad, the rhizome ...) does not consist of a negative indetermination or non-coincidence, instead it 'coincides' with a wholly positive force of self-

---

[19] J. Lacan, 'The Situation of Psychoanalysis and the Training of Psychoanalysts in 1956,' in Lacan 1966, 392.
[20] J. Lacan, 'Function and Field of Speech and Language in Psychoanalysis,' in Lacan 1966, 225–229; cf. Lacan 1956, 50; Dews 1987, 105.
[21] J. Lacan, 'Seminar on Purloined Letter,' in Lacan 1966, 21, 10.
[22] Ibid., 13.
[23] Lacan 1953, 16; Lacan 1955, 223.
[24] Cf. J. Lacan, 'Position of the Unconscious,' in Lacan 1966, 715.

differentiation. Deleuze and Guattari's schizophrenic "is not simply bisexual, or between the two, or intersexual. He is transexual. He is trans-parentchild [...]. He does not abolish disjunction by identifying the contradictory elements by means of elaboration; instead, he affirms it through a continuous overflight spanning an indivisible distance." The schizo does not inhabit the lack of a sexual relationship between 'man' and 'woman': "*he is himself this distance* that transforms him into a woman" (Deleuze & Guattari 1972, 76–77). More generally, Deleuze and Guattari insist, "one does not reach becoming or the molecular, as long as a line is connected to two distant points [...]. A becoming is neither the one nore the two, nor the relation of the two; it is the in-between [...], it constitutes a zone of proximity and indiscernibility, a no-man's land, a nonlocalisable relation sweeping up the two distant or contiguous points, carrying one into the proximity of the other" (Deleuze & Guattari 1980, 293). For the same reason, "you will not have reached the ultimate and irreducible terms of the unconscious so long as you find or restore a link [*lien*] between two elements" (Deleuze & Guattari 1972, 314).

In other words, Deleuze rejects the category of the subject for the same reason that Lacan embraces it. He rejects it as a dimension of negation and lack, on account of its radical disorientation, its exclusion from the domain of creation, being, or nature. When Deleuze affirms a version of Lacan's signifier or phallus, he reinterprets it as an instance of creative self-differentiation pure and simple (more on this below). When Deleuze affirms a version of Lacan's desire or speech, he deprives it precisely of its *subjective* dimension. In doing so, Deleuze makes a version of the mistake made by Foucault, when the latter claims an allegiance with Lacan insofar as he purportedly "shows how [...] structures, the very system of language itself—and not the subject—are what speak through the discourse of the patient and the symptoms of his neurosis," such that what speaks through the subject is simply an 'anonymous system without subject' (the 'anonymous murmur' of '*on parle*' or 'one speaks'): as Bertrand Ogilvie points out, such interpretations attribute to Lacan 'the opposite of what he says,' i.e. the effective elimination of the subject, its reduction to nothing more than a derivative 'nodal point in a network.'[25]

Consider for instance Deleuze and Lacan's respective understandings of the masochist 'subject,' for instance. Lacan associates 'primordial masochism' with the raw vulnerability of infant experience in its prematurity and dependence; masochism testifies to the fact that the human subject finds, in the 'earliest phase of misery that he goes through,' an anticipation of his death.[26] As far

---

[25] M. Foucault, Interview with *Quinzaine Littéraire*, 15 May 1966; cited in Ogilvie 1993, 42.
[26] J. Lacan, 'Presentation on Psychical Causality,' in Lacan 1966, 151–152.

as Deleuze is concerned, by contrast, the main interest of Leopold von Sacher-Masoch's writings is the way they illustrate the 'necessary joy in creation.' They demonstrate that "art is necessarily a liberation that explodes everything" (Deleuze 2002, 134). More specifically, they undertake a liberation from patriarchal subjectivity. Patriarchy functions here as a configuration of the symbolic family system in which the son is forced into a specific subject-position through identification with the father. The son is subjected via submission to the father. So whereas sadism negates or degrades the mother and exalts the punitive or castrating father, masochism begins, on the contrary, with the humiliation of the father. Masoch engineers situations in which "the father is excluded and completely nullified."[27] Inverting the famous Freudian fantasy, what is beaten and ridiculed in the masochist subject is not a child but rather the image of the father who oppresses that child. The immediate goal is to "obliterate the father's role and his likeness in order to generate the new man" (Deleuze 1967, 99). By excluding the father, Masoch invents a way of tapping into 'the great primary nature' which is in equal parts cold and sensual, impersonal and sentimental – the nature that expresses itself in 'the messianic idealism of the steppe' (Deleuze 1967, 54–55). By the same token, if a woman is never more sensual and exciting than when she is cold or inhuman (a statue, a painting, an ideal ...) this is because her coldness then excites a newly asexual sensuality and thus a liberation from desire-as-lack. What is new about Masoch's new man is his freedom from a dimension that psychoanalysis posits as constitutive of symbolic subjectivity itself – the constraints of genital sexuality. By liberating himself from desire oriented to the imperatives of reproduction and identity (and with it, from the constraints of family, property, work, the fatherland ...), our new man attains a 'state of mystical contemplation' and acquires the strength required 'to create a pure ideal reality' (Deleuze 1967, 33). The subtractive logic of such a process has little to do with the sort of subjective destitution championed by Lacan, or Slavoj Žižek. The masochist is not the person who comes to terms with a constitutive gap or lack, but rather the person who successfully hollows out a space of creative indetermination from within a psychological field that is otherwise always too full, too warm, too familiar.

The exclusion of the subject applies to its 'other' as well. According to Lacan, "language is constituted in such a way as to found us in the Other, while radically preventing us from understanding him."[28] The Other is the very locus (of speech or the symbolic) in which the subject, or intersubject, is

---

[27] Deleuze 1967, 61; cf. Deleuze 1961, 128; Deleuze 1993, 84–85.
[28] Lacan 1955, 286.

constituted; Laplanche radicalises this point, to make primary seduction by the Other the constituent principle of the unconscious itself.[29] For Deleuze too the other is a category of the (inter)subject, and for that very reason it is targeted for dissolution. The Other serves to integrate individuation and experience 'within the limits of objects and subjects' (Deleuze 1968a, 281). Far from disrupting the subject, the Other serves to consolidate and organise its perceptual and libidinal field. "I desire nothing that cannot be seen, thought, or possessed by a possible Other" (Deleuze 1969, 306), and "the fundamental effect [of the Other] is the distinction of my consciousness and its object"; by the same token, "the absence of the Other is felt when we bang against things, when the stupefying swiftness of our actions is revealed to us ..."[30] In order to grasp the immediate intensity of things, we must therefore strive to "reach those regions where the Other-structure no longer functions, far from the objects and subjects that it conditions, where singularities are free to be deployed or distributed within pure Ideas, and individuating factors to be distributed in pure intensity" (Deleuze 1968a, 282). In the absence of the Other, "the whole of our perceived world collapses in the interest of something else" (Deleuze 1969, 310), namely, Reality. "In the Other's absence, consciousness and its object are one. There is no longer any possibility of error." Liberated from the Other, "consciousness ceases to be a light cast upon objects in order to become a pure phosphorescence of things in themselves" (Deleuze 1969, 311), and the things themselves are returned to their 'natural' state – the regime of constant variation in which all "elements are released and renewed, having become celestial and forming a thousand capricious elemental figures," tracing a *ligne de fuite* that might allow "the entire earth to escape" (Deleuze 1969, 312).

3. Along with the other, the subject, and the intersubject, Deleuze refuses the process of representation

The 'naturalism' that Deleuze affirms after Spinoza and Leibniz acknowledges only a single dimension of reality, a single plane of consistency or creation, a single 'machinic-nature.' There is "only one kind of production, the production

---

[29] "The unconscious is only maintained in its radical alterity by the other person (*der Andere*): in brief, by seduction" – conventionally, the enigmatic seduction of the child by its mother (Laplanche 1999, 71). Acknowledgement of the unconscious demands that we "recognise in us the existence of a foreign body hard as iron" (J. Laplanche, 'Short Treatise,' in Laplanche 1999, 114).

[30] Deleuze 1969, 306. "The mistake of theories of knowledge is that they postulate the contemporaneity of subject and object, whereas one is constituted only through the annihilation of the other" (310).

of the real" (Deleuze & Guattari 1972, 32). If being is creating or differing, if desire is immediately productive and affirmative, if all of reality *is* in one and the same sense, then representation simply obstructs our intuition of and participation in that reality. For this reason an unqualified critique of the 'long error of representation' is one of the great constants of Deleuze's work, and it is common to all of his own philosophical ancestors.[31] Filtered through representation, desire ceases to be immediate or productive so as to become merely figurative or symbolic, a matter for interpretation, an illusion made up only of language, dream, or myth. Oedipus plays a crucial role in this process. Thanks to Oedipus, "the whole of desiring-production is crushed, subjected to the requirements of representation." This is indeed the "essential thing: the reproduction of desire gives way to a simple representation [...]. Every time that production, rather than being apprehended in its originality, in its reality, becomes reduced in this manner to a representational space, it can no longer have value except by its own absence, and it appears as a lack within this space" (Deleuze & Guattari 1972, 54, 306).

On the other hand, when Lacan says that a "signifier represents a subject for another signifier" he blocks any immediately expressive or productive conception of desire, being, or reality.[32] He also, as Alenka Zupančič explains, provides the basis for 'an entirely new conception of representation.' The signifier does not serve here to name objects for a subject, any more than it represents in a stable or definitive way a subject for another subject. A subject does not represent itself; its existence depends upon a medium that it does not control. The subject cannot coincide with itself. A subject is caught up in the endless referral of signifier to signifier to signifier ... The signifier that represents a subject does not do so by analogy or approximation, it does not more or less 'mis-represent' the true being or nature of a subject. Instead it opens up the 'excessive' space of a subject in the interval between signifiers. Such "representation is itself infinite and constitutively not-all (or non-conclusive), it represents no object [...]. Here, representation as such is a wandering excess over itself; representation *is* the infinite tarrying with the excess that springs— not simply from what is or is not represented (its 'object'), but from this act of representation itself, from its own inherent 'crack' or inconsistency."[33]

---

[31] Deleuze 1968a, 301. The whole of "Hume's philosophy is a sharp critique of representation" (Deleuze 1953, 30); Nietzsche reduces representation to a component of 'slave' psychology (Deleuze 1962, 10); Bergson finds in representation the root of our misunderstanding of memory, if not of all our metaphysical confusion (Deleuze 2002, 29); Spinoza distinguishes between the univocal expression of an adequate idea from its equivocal and approximate representation (Deleuze 1968b, 56–57).

[32] J. Lacan, 'The Subversion of the Subject and the Dialectic of Desire,' in Lacan 1966, 694.

[33] Zupančič 2004, 199.

4. Along with representation, Deleuze also rejects the primacy of signification and the symbolic

This rejection amounts to a refusal of Lacan's most basic intuition, his insistence that "words are the only material of the unconscious", that "is the world of words that creates the world of things—things which at first run together in the *hic et nunc* of the all in the process of becoming—by giving its concrete being to their essence."[34] As Žižek and Zupančič have repeatedly argued, Lacan's Real is not a form of being external to signification, some sort of 'hard kernel' that representation can only misrepresent. The Real is itself a dimension of representation and signification. "The Real is not something outside or beyond representation," Zupančič continues, "but is the very crack of representation,"[35] the dimension of its constitutive incompleteness.

Deleuze and Guattari's productive desiring-machines, by contrast, "represent nothing, signify nothing, mean nothing, and are exactly what one makes of them, what is made with them, what they make in themselves" (Deleuze & Guattari 1972, 288). One way or another, desiring-machines or becomings provide forms of access to a domain "of pure intensities that are valuable only in themselves, where all forms come undone, as do all the significations, signifiers, and signifieds, to the benefit of an unformed matter of deterritorialised flux."[36] Writing and language can have no privileged role in the production of such a domain, and are included in it only insofar as they no longer signify reality but participate in its production: if there is writing, it must be 'flush with the real' (Deleuze & Guattari 1972, 87), such that "writing now functions on the same level as the real, and the real materially writes."[37]

From a Deleuzian perspective, signification is simply another obstacle that must be removed if we are to grasp an appropriately immediate intuition of reality. Signification is one of the mechanisms through which we remain trapped in our ignorance of reality; along with the organism and the subject, it is one of the fundamental forms of our stratification or territorialisation. What matters in a Deleuzian universe is the creation or production of something,

---

[34] J. Lacan, 'Of Structure as the Inmixing of an Otherness Prerequisite to Any Subject Whatever,' in Lacan 1970, 187; J. Lacan, 'Function and Field of Speech and Language in Psychoanalysis,' in Lacan 1966, 229.
[35] Zupančič 2004, 199.
[36] Deleuze & Guattari 1975, 13. 'The becoming-animal of the human being is real, even if the animal the human being becomes is not [...]. You do not become a barking molar dog, but by barking, if it is done with enough feeling, with enough necessity and composition, you emit a molecular dog' (Deleuze & Guattari 1980, 238, 275).
[37] Deleuze & Guattari 1980, 141; cf. 512; Deleuze 1993, 11.

not its representation or signification. This is why what Deleuze calls "sense [*sens*] is not to be confused with signification; sense is rather what is attributed in such a way that it determines both the signifier and the signified as such" (Deleuze 1969, 50–51). As a facet of univocal being or creation, "sense brings that which expresses it into existence" (166). Sense is nothing less than the immediate expression of being itself, and as such is "something unconditioned, capable of assuring a real genesis of denotation and of the other dimensions of the proposition" (19). It is this sort of immediate and *absolute* expression that Deleuze tries to attribute to Lacan's own version of signification when he considers the logic of the 'Purloined Letter' or the phallic signifier in terms of a differing 'object = x.' Differentiated structures are shaped, "above all, by the nature of the object = x that presides over their functioning." Given a structured situation made up of differentiated elements, Deleuze argues,

> it is in relation to [this] object that the variety of terms and the variation of differential relations are determined in each case [...]. The *relative* places of the terms in the structure depend first on the *absolute* place of each, at least moment, in relation to the object = x that is always circulating, always displaced in relation to itself [...]. Distributing the differences through the entire structure, making the differential relations vary with its displacements, the object = x constitutes the differenciating element of difference itself. (Deleuze 2002, 185–186)

According to Deleuze's reading, Lacan's concept of the phallus is precisely that which "founds sexuality *in its entirety* as system or structure, and in relation to which the places occupied by men and women are distributed." All by itself, this phallus "determines the relative place of the elements and the variable value of relations."[38]

5. *Ultimately, there is no place in a Deleuzian universe for a psychoanalytic conception of the unconscious itself*

Or at least, there is no place here for a distinctively Lacanian notion of the unconscious, an unconscious structured like a language and grounded in the alterity and exteriority of the symbolic. According to Lacan, we speak with words that 'escape our vigilance,' words whose signification we do not control.

---

[38] Deleuze 2002, 186–188. "As a general rule, the real, the imaginary and their relations are always engendered secondarily by the functioning of the structure, which starts by having its primary effect in itself" (Deleuze 2002, 191).

It is precisely as a result of its lack of any natural (or instinctual) orientation that the unconscious is forever irreducible to consciousness. If nature itself thinks, then 'thought is always there' and thought, like instinct, would be naturally prepared by life. If thought is a natural process, then the unconscious is without difficulty. But the unconscious has nothing to do with instinct or primitive knowledge or preparation of thought in some underground. It is a thinking with words, with thoughts that escape your vigilance.[39]

Now, although Deleuze repeatedly says that "thought thinks only on the basis of an unconscious"[40] or that "the sole subject of reproduction is the unconscious itself" (Deleuze & Guattari 1972, 108), his understanding of this unconscious is based precisely on an essential continuity between nature or cosmos and thought. It is precisely the "coextension of man and nature" that underlies the "circular movement by which the unconscious, always remaining subject, produces and reproduces itself" (Deleuze & Guattari 1972, 107). Again, if "there is only involuntary thought" (Deleuze 1968a, 139), if thinking is never the willed or deliberate activity of a given organism or species, this is because thinking expresses the very being of reality or nature itself. According to Deleuze's Spinozist conception of things, "we have a power of knowing, understanding or thinking only to the extent that we participate in the absolute power of thinking" (Deleuze 1968b, 142), and this power of thinking is a facet of being itself. Being thinks, being thinks through beings. The Deleuzian unconscious is nothing other than a thinking that articulates 'brain and cosmos' in a single intensity or non-organic life (Deleuze 1985, 215; cf. 151). The 'cosmos-brain' has all of the characteristics of pure creation as such, and is formally indistinguishable from a pantheistic 'super-consciousness.'

> It is an absolute consistent form that surveys itself independently of any supplementary dimension, which does not appeal therefore to any dimension, which has only a single side whatever the number of its dimensions, which remains copresent to all its determinations without proximity or distance, traverses them at infinite speed, without limit-speed, and which makes of them so many inseparable variations on which it confers an equipotentiality without confusion. (Deleuze & Guattari 1991, 210; cf. Deleuze & Guattari 1980, 343–347)

---

[39] Lacan 1970, 189.
[40] Deleuze 1964, 99; Deleuze 1968a, 85–86, 199, 194; cf. Deleuze 1963, viii–ix.

If there is an analogue within the psychoanalytic tradition to Deleuze's conception of the cosmos-brain it is not Lacan's unconscious, but rather Jung's cosmic consciousness.[41]

Bibliography

Althusser, L. 1964. 'Freud and Lacan.' In *Lenin and Philosophy*. London: New Left Books, 1971.

Bergson, H. 1896. *Matter and Memory*. Translated by N. M. Paul and W. S. Palmer. New York: Zone Books, 1988.

———. 1907. *Creative Evolution*. Translated by A. Mitchell. New York: Henry Holt, 1911.

———. 1932. *The Two Sources of Morality and Religion*. Translated by R. Ashley Audra and C. Brereton. With W. Horsfall Carter. New York: Doubleday, 1954.

Deleuze, G. 1953. *Empiricism and Subjectivity*. Translated by C. Boundas. New York: Columbia University Press, 1991.

———. 1961. 'From Sacher-Masoch to Masochism.' Translated by C. Kerslake. *Angelaki* 9, no.1 (April 2004): 125–133.

———. 1962. *Nietzsche and Philosophy*. Translated by H. Tomlinson. Minneapolis: University of Minnesota Press, 1983.

———. 1963. *Kant's Critical Philosophy*. Translated by H. Tomlinson and B. Habberjam. Minneapolis: University of Minnesota Press, 1984.

———. 1964. *Proust and Signs*. Translated by R. Howard. London: Continuum, 2000.

———. 1966. *Bergsonism*. Translated by H. Tomlinson and B. Habberjam. New York: Zone Books, 1988.

———. 1967. *Masochism: An Interpretation of Coldness and Cruelty*. Translated by J. McNeil. New York: Zone Books, 1989.

———. 1968a. *Difference and Repetition*. Translated by P. Patton. New York: Columbia University Press, 1994.

---

[41] "Like every other being," writes Jung, "I am a splinter of the infinite deity." Rather like Bergson before him, Jung believes that "man is indispensable for the completion of creation; that, in fact, he himself is the second creator of the world." Rather like Deleuze and Guattari after him, Jung affirms a distinctively 'rhizomatic' vitalism: "Life has always seemed to me like a plant that lives on its rhizome. Its true life is invisible, hidden in the rhizome. The part that appears above ground lasts only a single summer. Then it withers away – an ephemeral apparition. When we think of the unending growth and decay of life and civilizations, we cannot escape the impression of absolute nullity. Yet I have never lost a sense of something that lives and endures beneath the eternal flux. What we see is the blossom, which passes. The rhizome remains" (Jung 1961, 17–18). The link between Deleuze and Jung has recently been explored in detail in Kerslake 2007.

———. 1968b. *Expressionism in Philosophy: Spinoza.* Translated by M. Joughin. New York: Zone Books, 1990.

———. 1969. *The Logic of Sense.* Translated by M. Lester and C. Stivale. New York: Columbia University Press, 1990.

———. 1977. *Dialogues.* Translated by H. Tomlinson and B. Habberjam. New York: Columbia University Press, 1987.

———. 1983. *Cinema 1: The Movement-Image.* Translated by H. Tomlinson and B. Habberjam. Minneapolis: University of Minnesota Press, 1986.

———. 1985. *Cinema 2: The Time-Image.* Translated by H. Tomlinson and R. Galeta Minneapolis: University of Minnesota Press, 1989.

———. 1986. *Foucault.* Translated by S. Hand. Minneapolis: University of Minnesota Press, 1988.

———. 1990. *Negotiations.* Translated by M. Joughin. New York: Columbia University Press, 1995.

———. 1993. *Essays Critical and Clinical.* Translated by D. W. Smith and M. A. Greco. Minneapolis: University of Minnesota Press, 1997.

———. 2001. *Pure Immanence: Essays on a Life.* New York: Zone Books, 2001.

———. 2002. *Desert Islands and Other Texts 1953–1974.* Translated by M. Taormina. Cambridge, MA: Semiotext(e), 2004.

———. 2003. *Deux Régimes de fous. Textes et entretiens 1975–1995.* Edited by D. Lapoujade. Paris: Editions de Minuit, 2003.

Deleuze, G., and F. Guattari. 1972. *Anti-Oedipus.* Translated by R. Hurley, M. Seem, and H. R. Lane. Minneapolis: University of Minnesota Press, 1977.

———. 1975. *Kafka: For a Minor Literature.* Translated by D. Polan. Minneapolis: University of Minnesota Press, 1986.

———. 1980. *A Thousand Plateaus.* Translated by B. Massumi. Minneapolis: University of Minnesota Press, 1986.

———. 1991. *What is Philosophy?* Translated by H. Tomlinson and G. Burchell. New York: Columbia University Press, 1994.

Dews, Peter. 1987. *Logics of Disintegration.* London: Verso, 1987.

Jung, C. G. 1961. *Memories, Dreams, Reflections.* Edited by A. Jaffé. Translated by C. Winston and R. Winston. New York: Vintage, 1989.

Kerslake, C. 2007. *Deleuze and the Unconscious.* London: Continuum, 2007.

Lacan, J. 1951. 'Some Reflections on the Ego.' *International Journal of Psychoanalysis* 34 (1953), pp. 11-17.

———. 1954. *Seminar I: Freud's Papers on Technique* [1953–1954]. Translated by J. Forrester. New York: Norton, 1988.

———. 1955. *Seminar II: The Ego in Freud's Theory and in the Technique of Psychoanalysis* [1954–1955]. Translated by S. Tomaselli. New York: Norton, 1988.

———. 1956. *Seminar III: The Psychoses.* Translated by R. Grigg. London: Routledge, 1988.

———. 1966. *Écrits.* Translated by B. Fink. New York: Norton, 2006.

———. 1970. 'Of Structure as the Inmixing of an Otherness Prerequisite to Any Subject Whatever.' In *The Languages of Criticism and the Sciences of Man: The Structuralist Controversy*, edited by R. A. Macksey and E. Donato. Baltimore: Johns Hopkins University Press, 1970.

Laplanche, J. 1999. *Essays on Otherness*. Edited by J. Fletcher. London: Routledge, 1999.

Ogilvie, B. 1993. *Lacan: Le Sujet*. Paris: PUF, 1993.

Zupančič, A. 2004. 'The Fifth Condition.' In *Think Again: Badiou and the Future of Philosophy*, edited by P. Hallward. London: Continuum, 2004, pp. 191-201.

Desire and the Dialectics of Love: Deleuze, Canguilhem, and the Philosophy of Desire

Christian Kerslake

Deleuze and the Philosophy of Desire

In the section on 'Desire' in his 1980s television interviews with Claire Parnet (*The ABC of Gilles Deleuze*), Deleuze expresses regret about misunderstandings generated by the notion of desire in *Anti-Oedipus*, which, he says, was "meant to express the simplest thing in the world," but instead ended up suggesting to many a simplistic affirmation of brute, immediate 'spontaneity.' It is indeed a strange situation when a concept that apparently expresses 'the simplest thing in the world,' becomes so dangerously open to misunderstanding. A genealogy of the concept of desire in Deleuze's work is therefore called for. For, although Deleuze is indeed popularly known as a 'philosopher of desire,' the concept of desire only emerges very gradually, in fits and starts, in his early work. In his main philosophical work, *Difference and Repetition* (1968), there is only one brief discussion of the concept of desire. Until 1972, with the publication of *Anti-Oedipus*, most references to the concept of desire in Deleuze's writings occur specifically in the context of his reading of Proust, presented most completely in *Proust and Signs* (1964).

Deleuze's ideas about desire in his work on Proust, however, first emerge within the context of a philosophy of love. In attempting to clarify the notion of desire in the late television interviews, he returns to these same ideas about the specifically 'amorous' features of desire. It is not that there is a critique of desire as 'lack' already present in Proust, he suggests, but rather that there is in Proust a very important transformation of the notion of the *object* of desire, which in effect supersedes traditional notions of *what* is desired in the process of desire. For Proust, "the desire for a woman is not so much a desire for the woman as for a landscape, an environment, that is enveloped in this woman" (Deleuze & Parnet 1997, 'Desire'). To desire is not to desire an 'object,' but *to be drawn into another world expressed by that object*. The object is not desirable in itself, but nor is it desirable because it substitutes for a lost former object, or because it enfolds a void (as Freudian and Lacanian psychoanalysis have it). Instead, its desirability is to be found in its expressive qualities, and in their status as an envelope for self-differentiation. For Proust, the aim of desire is to enter another world through an object. For the early and late Deleuze alike, desire is not separable from imagination, which is responsible for carrying desire towards its object and, through it, into the 'world' it harbours within it. Even and especially in children and schizophrenics, desire seeks *another world* in the object, a world that is folded up and implicated within the desired being. With his reference to Proust in the *ABC*, Deleuze indicates that the first approach to the notion of desire should be sought in the lover who seeks another world in and through the body of another.

A genealogy of the concept of desire in Deleuze which stressed the importance of the theory of love in *Proust and Signs* would take us far from standard psychoanalytic ideas about desire from the Freudian or Lacanian traditions. This would not be so surprising from within the context of Deleuze's intellectual formation in the 1950s. In the period before Lacan rose to pre-eminence, Bergsonian, Janetian, and Proustian philosophies of love still suffused French culture and thought; Deleuze's early essay 'Description of a Woman' (1946) arises from that context. In the following essay, I am going to appeal to a text on the philosophy of desire published in 1952 by Georges Canguilhem, and which I am going to hypothesise influenced Deleuze. Canguilhem's *Besoins et Tendances (Needs and Tendencies)* was the first in a series of *Textes et Documents Philosophiques* (of which Canguilhem was also the general editor) published by Hachette, and in which Deleuze's own edited collection, *Instincts and Institutions*, appeared as the second volume in 1953. Deleuze refers to Canguilhem's volume both explicitly and implicitly in his own volume, and gives the impression that *Instincts and Institutions* is built on the more elementary foundations laid out in the first volume.[42] It turns out that the matrix for Deleuze's Proustian ideas about desire, along with the materials for his later critique of desire as lack and negativity, are already latent in a chapter of Canguilhem's volume, entitled 'Philosophical

---

[42] Cf. Deleuze 1953, 13. For an important implicit reference, see the subheading to Deleuze's chapter on 'Institution,' which gives a preliminary definition of institution as a "system of indirect and social means for satisfying a tendency" (1), while his chapter on 'Instinct' gives a complementary definition of instinct as a "system of direct and specific means for satisfying a tendency" (18). Here we are implicitly referred back to Canguilhem's volume for a definition of 'tendency.'

Analysis of Tendency and Desire.'[43] Although not much is said there about what a 'tendency' might be, Canguilhem's whole chapter is taken up with an interesting selection and organisation of a series of philosophical texts on desire, centred around one of the very texts by Proust that will later exert its power over Deleuze in his theory of desire. Canguilhem orders the texts under a series of headings:

1. Desire and its complementary object (Plato, Spinoza, Augustine/ Jean Nogué).
2. Amorous desire and its proper aim (Proust).
3. Disquiet [*l'inquiétude*] in desire (Leibniz).
4. Negativity in desire according to Hegel (Jean Hyppolite).
5. Desire as lack and the transcendence of lack (Sartre).

The present essay follows the order of Canguilhem's selection, which, as we will see, is ordered by an inner logic. What most strikes the reader today about the section on 'Tendency and Desire' in Canguilhem's *Besoins et tendances* is how he has framed the selections in terms of an opposition between positive and negative desire, desire as positive affect versus desire as lack. Canguilhem's book rests on a familiar distinction between need and desire. With desire, it seems, we transcend biologically pre-programmed relations of need. But the treatment of desire here is quite different from the discussion found in Freud's 'Drives and their Vicissitudes,' with its distinctions between aim, object, source, and pressure. Instead we begin with Plato and Spinoza, each weighing in with their definition of desire, after which Augustine steps in to reconcile the two views. Then we turn to Proust, whose introduction of the factor of love problematises Freud's distinction between aim and object. From Proust, we go to Leibniz (in *Proust and Signs* Deleuze makes a version of the same journey), and then we are finally able to assess philosophically the question of the negativity or positivity of desire. In Canguilhem's text, the most elementary questions about desire are raised, in the raw form of passages from the history of philosophy, unmediated by contemporary ideas or confusions about the nature of desire. If desire is a 'tendency' for Canguilhem, this must

---

[43] 'Tendency,' in effect, seems to include whatever cannot be straightforwardly classed as a physiological or biological need. The difference between need and tendency seems to be a way of articulating the classic psychoanalytic distinction between need and drive, without explicitly endorsing psychoanalytic claims about the content involved in the distinction. This proximity of tendency and drive also seems to be supported by Canguilhem's subsequent citations from Freud, where Freud's *Trieb* (drive) is mostly also translated as *tendance*. Canguilhem presents three extracts from the 1923 French translation of Freud's *Introductory Lectures on Psychoanalysis* (by S. Jankélévitch, authorised by Freud). It thus turns out that it is a myth that Freud's notion of drive was everywhere confused with the notion of instinct before Lacan came along. *Trieb* first appeared in French as *tendance*, not as *instinct*.

be because there is a question about what it tends toward: does it aim at an intrinsically satisfying object, or is the object merely the pretext for its aim? Does sexual desire have a pre-given object, or does the object stand in as a pretext for the intrinsic satisfaction of a deeper aim? What end is being sought in sexual activity? What is the relationship between sexual desire and love? By exploring these works of Canguilhem and Deleuze, we will be able to return to the contribution of the philosophical tradition to the theory of desire, love, and their mutual intrication.

Desire and its Object: Plato, Spinoza, and Augustine

The first section of the abovementioned chapter deals with 'Desire and its complementary object' and comprises texts by Plato, Spinoza and a French phenomenologist, Jean Nogué (who discusses Augustine). It can be understood as laying out two opposed conceptions of desire (Platonic and Spinozist), and then moving towards an 'Augustinian' synthesis of the two. The extract from Plato is from his discussion in the *Republic* of the three parts of the soul – appetite (*epithumia*), reason (*logos*) and spirit (*thumos*). Socrates is depicted contending that there is a basic sense in which "each desire is directed simply towards its own natural object, and any qualification is an addition" (*Republic* 437e). When we are thirsty, we simply want a drink, and any special virtues of the particular drink we eventually have are additional to the basic desire. Canguilhem adds a reference to Plato's *Meno* where Socrates states that, in any case, nobody knowingly desires an object that is not good (*Meno* 77b-78b). Taken together, these two Platonic texts suggest a particular conception of the object of desire as something natural and good. Desire is therefore defined through its object, which is seen as pre-given and complementary, in accordance with Platonic idealism in general.

This conception is then counterposed to Spinoza's theory of desire in Book III of the *Ethics*. Each thing, says Spinoza, 'as far as it can by its own power' exhibits a striving (*conatus*) to 'persevere in its being' (E III P6). "When this striving is related only to the mind, it is called will, but when it is related to the mind and body together, it is called appetite"; and when, further, the mind is conscious of its appetite, through its ideas about its bodily affections, this is called desire: "*Desire* can be defined as *appetite together with the consciousness of the appetite*" (E III P9 Schol.). Spinoza later goes so far as to say that 'desire is man's very essence' (E III, Definitions of the Affects, I). But lest this be taken in any vitalistic sense, he qualifies this definition by making clear that desire is only man's essence because it is the vehicle by which he is 'determined to do something': Desire is man's very essence, "insofar as it is conceived to be determined, from any given affection, to do something." Human bodies are affected (through both internal and external stimuli), and have certain ideas about what they are affected by and how they should respond to their affections. But their responses to these affections are always determined in the last instance by their striving to 'persevere in their own being,' 'as far as they can by their own power.' They desire what is good *for them*, what helps them preserve themselves, rather than what is held to be intrinsically good. Spinoza concludes, in the section quoted by Canguilhem, "[I]t is clear that we neither strive for, nor will, neither want, nor desire anything because we judge it to be good; on the contrary, we judge something to be good because we strive for it, will it, want it, desire it" (E III P9 Schol.).

In his *Spinoza: Practical Philosophy*, Deleuze emphasises that if 'self-preservation' seems to be at the heart of Spinoza's argument here, this is meant in a very specific sense, as is indicated by Spinoza's mention of the role of *power*. If we restrict Spinoza's claims to organisms, we can make his argument more concrete. We must conceive of each organic body as having certain powers. But its power to do something also corresponds to a feeling of that power, so that "all power is inseparable from a capacity for being affected" (Deleuze 1981, 97). To have a power is to have power *over* other things (whether it be one's own emotions, one's reactions, or other people). However, "there is no singular thing in nature than which there is not another more powerful and stronger" (E IV, Axiom). The organic body is in a relation of power with many things in its environment, in such a way that the whole of nature can be seen as composed of power relations, with each being having its own internal thresholds, beyond which it loses its struggle to preserve its place. But this notion of power allows us to get beyond the idea of self-preservation as the preservation of a stable state. For the world is populated by things that either increase or diminish our power of acting, that weaken our power or increase its range and subtlety: "By *joy*, therefore, I shall understand in what follows that *passion by which the mind passes to a greater perfection*. And by *sadness*, that *passion by which it passes to a lesser perfection*" (E III P11). In these terms, Deleuze says, "the *conatus* is the effort to experience joy, to increase the power of acting, to imagine and find that which is a cause of joy, which maintains and furthers this cause; and also an effort to avert sadness, to imagine and find that which destroys the cause of sadness" (Deleuze 1981, 101).

We can see that these two texts in Canguilhem's collection are opposites: for Plato, desire is defined as the seeking of a good object, whereas, for

Spinoza, the goodness of the object of desire is referred back to the fact that one desires whatever will increase one's power. In one case, the tendency of desire is to find an appropriate, pre-given *object*; the object is the aim of desire. In the other, desire tends towards the *aim* of increasing the power of the organism; the object is secondary to the aim. This opposition between Plato and Spinoza inverts Freud's famous historical distinction between two types of desire in *Three Essays on the Theory of Sexuality*: he remarks that "the most striking distinction between the erotic life of antiquity and our own no doubt lies in the fact that the ancients laid the stress on the drive itself, whereas we emphasise the object"; where the ancients glorified the drive itself, we "despise the activity of the drive itself, and find excuses for it only in the merits of the object" (SE 7, 149). We have been seeing how it is Plato, the ancient, who gives primacy to the object, and Spinoza, the modern, who emphasises the activity of desiring, which could here equally be described as its tendency or drive.

The final text, by Jean Nogué, can be understood as a kind of dialectical supersession of the first two. Nogué cites the opening of Book III of Augustine's *Confessions*, where Augustine recalls how, in youth, "I was not yet in love, but was in love with love ... I was looking for something to love, since I was in love with loving." For Nogué, Augustine is suggesting how "the object of the tendency (of amorous desire) can precede the person in whom it is fixed ... The sensible idol is just the pretext of the object that desire seeks" (Canguilhem 1952, 46).[44] Augustine testifies to a primary desire to desire (or a desire to be in love with something), which first seeks out an object fit to play the role of being desired. Nogué's text suggests that it is the *aim* that is pre-given, rather than the object. Desire has a tendency to fulfil a particular aim, and seeks an object that can serve as the vessel for the attainment of that aim. Canguilhem then appends a note to Nogué's citation of Augustine which asks us to refer on to the next section, 'Amorous Desire and its Proper Aim,' which contains a sole text, by Proust. The text, from *In the Shadow of Young Girls in Flower*, a volume of Proust's *In Search of Lost Time* (Proust 1919, 368–375; with some paragraphs omitted), is thus presented as the truth of the previous texts.

In the first movement of Canguilhem's presentation of the philosophy of desire, the Augustinian model of desire reconciled Platonic and Spinozist desire. Even if it is desire that determines what is good, rather than vice versa (as in Plato), Spinoza's desire is experienced as pre-given, unfolding from a pre-existent essence. To that extent, Spinoza's theory of *conatus* can indeed be called 'recollective.' In *Difference and Repetition*, it would seem that Deleuze's

---

[44] The passage is from Nogué's *La Signification du Sensible* (Nogué 1936, 29–31).

model of desire incorporates the Platonic and Augustinian notions about the primacy of the object of desire. His aim is to show how desire, and amorous desire in particular, is ultimately structured in terms of repetition; and the ultimate goal of repetition is to overcome recollection. Nevertheless, there *is* a sense in which Spinozist desire can be defended, if it is taken up again in the light of Proust's reflections on love. Canguilhem's presentation of desire from Spinoza to Proust, and then to Sartre's critique of Spinoza, bears within it another possible lesson. In fact, it is as if Deleuze goes on to follow up the trajectory from Spinoza to Proust and Leibniz. Let us retrace the movement.

Proust and the Proper Object of Sexual Desire

In the passage, Marcel is remembering a period of youth when

> the idle heart, unoccupied with love for a particular person, lies in wait for Beauty, seeking it everywhere, as the man in love sees and desires in all things the woman he cherishes. We need only to see in passing a single real feature of a woman, a glimpse of her at a distance or from behind, which can be enough for us to project Beauty on to her, and we imagine we have found it at last: the heart beats faster, we lengthen our stride and, on condition that she disappears, we may be left with the certainty of having set eyes upon her—it is only if we succeed in catching up with her that we discover our mistake. (Proust 1919, 368)

It is this passage to which Canguilhem refers, as if it provides the perfect example of the Augustinian suggestion that desire has a pre-given tendency to fulfil a particular aim, and seeks an object that can serve as the vessel for the attainment of that aim. Desire only needs a 'single real feature' to serve as material for the 'projection' of the ideal. Marcel is intensely fascinated by the beautifully dressed women and girls who seem to be everywhere in the resort of Balbec, but says, "I did not recognise that, underlying my curiosity about them, there was a desire for possession [*désir de possession*]" (Proust 1919, 368). Because it involves a projection onto the other, this desire for possession is simultaneously the desire *of* possession, in person, as it were. The subject never truly leaves itself in this desire, and ultimately treats all others in the Platonic manner, as a cause for reminiscence. Augustine's conception of desire is only different from Plato's insofar as the aim of desire is pre-existent rather than the object itself. If by making this modification Augustine can proleptically answer the Spinozist charge, this is only to recapture desire in the embrace of reminiscence.

Nevertheless, although the beginning of the text from Proust does indeed exemplify the Augustinian concept of desire, the ensuing passages unfold this premise in an unexpected direction. The desire for possession is superseded when desire is transformed into 'amorous desire.' Desire falls from its position of wanting to possess into a new position, that of love. Canguilhem's title for the extract suggests that the 'proper object' of the type of desire involved in love is different from that of desire in general. It is not that love does not involve the desire for possession (far from it); it is, rather, that the discovery of the proper object of amorous desire deepens the desire for possession so that something else—the *end* of love—emerges from its shadow. We will see towards the end of this section that Deleuze's own exploration of the logic of desire can be explicated through this movement from Spinoza, through Augustine, to Proust. There is thus a secret path to be discovered between Deleuze's work on Spinoza and Proust—the path of a positive notion of desire, which evolves through the experience of love, in contradistinction to the conception of desire as negative, which remains on the shores of the mere desire for possession. We will cite liberally from the rest of Proust's text, not least because it contains passages that will be extremely important for Deleuze.

> Then he sees 'five or six' young girls walking along the esplanade, one with her bicycle, others carrying golf-clubs, dressed in a manner quite different from the other girls at the resort. For an instant, as I passed close to the brunette with the full cheeks and the bicycle, I glimpsed her oblique, laughing glance, looking out from the inhumane world which circumscribed the life of their little tribe [*la vie de cette petite tribu*], an inaccessible *terra incognita*, obviously incapable of harbouring or offering a home to any notion of who or what I was. With her toque pulled down low on her brow, entirely engrossed in what her companions were saying, did she see me, at the moment when the black ray from her eyes encountered me? If so, what must I have seemed like to her? What sort of world was the one from which she was looking at me? I could not tell, any more than one can tell from the few details which a telescope enables us to descry on a neighbouring planet whether it is inhabited by human beings, whether or not they can see us, or whether their view of us has inspired any reflections in them. (Proust 1919, 374; last sentence not included in Canguilhem)

Proust then reflects on what lies behind the eyes of this girl: "whatever it is that shines in those reflective discs is not reducible to their material composition; ... flitting about behind them are the black incognizable shadows of the ideas she forms about the people and places she knows—the paddocks at race-courses, the sandy paths along which she might have pedalled, drawing me after her, over hill and meadow ... her own impenetrable projects and the designs of others upon her" (375). He then qualifies what he had said earlier about the desire for possession: "I knew I could never possess the young cyclist, unless I could also possess what lay behind her eyes. My desire for her was desire for her whole life." Suddenly his desire for possession is transformed in nature. He knows that there is nothing in the life of the girls with which he has any familiarity, or to which he knows how to gain access. His desire is now "full of pain, because I sensed it was unattainable." But it was also full of excitement, because all that has been his life up until that moment falls away, and he feels his life has turned around a corner into a great space, "which I longed to explore and which was composed of the lives led by these young girls, because what was laid out now before my eyes was that extension and potential multiplication of self which we know as happiness" (375).

This passage, which recounts Marcel's first encounter with Albertine, seems to have deeply influenced Deleuze. It is essential to the Leibnizian interpretation of love as the encounter with a 'possible world' in *Proust and Signs* (Deleuze 1964, 7–8), where Deleuze uses Proust's reflection as the key to the process of love. First, the beloved appears as a *sign* that captivates and draws the lover towards him or her for reasons he or she does not understand: "The beloved appears as a sign, a 'soul'; the beloved expresses a possible world unknown to us, implying, enveloping, imprisoning a world that must be deciphered, that is interpreted" (7). 'Sign' appears here in the mantic sense of an 'omen,' a secret sign directed solely at the lover, which seems to say 'follow me.' The beloved's dress, accent, gestures all seem to express a way of seeing the world that is completely *individual*: "to fall in love is to individualise someone by the signs he bears or emits" (7). But the beloved gains the power to draw us into the 'depth' which she or he envelops only because she or he is *looking at us* from within the world that she or he inhabits. First, she or he expresses a world, but second, we are displaced from our own world, because she or he is seeing us from within hers or his: "How can we gain access to a landscape that is no longer the one we see, but on the contrary the one in which we are seen?" (8).

But the Proust text is also essential to the culminating paragraphs on the interiorisation of difference in *Difference and Repetition*. For Deleuze, the encounter with the Other as a possible world opens up the highest, most 'implicated' form of difference, and is the privilege of 'psychic systems.' It is the apex of self-differentiation, insofar as it is an internalisation of difference or otherness which simultaneously opens the interiority of the subject out onto other possible worlds. The other "endows the possibles that it expresses with reality, independently of the development that we cause them to undergo" (Deleuze 1968, 261). Deleuze invokes a 'rule' for this state of affairs: "not to explicate oneself too much with the other, not to explicate the other too much, but to maintain one's implicit values and multiply one's own world by populating it with all those expressed that do not exist apart from their expressions" (261). The final words of *Difference and Repetition* (before the Conclusion of the book, which is a summary), are: "The structure of the other and the corresponding function of language effectively represent the manifestation of the noumenon, the appearance of expressive values—in short, the tendency towards the interiorisation of difference" (261). Thus Proust's text provides Deleuze with the blueprint for a philosophy of love, as well as with the materials that he needs to close his philosophical system at the speculative level. When Marcel falls in love, he really does see "laid out now before [his] eyes ... that extension and potential multiplication of self which we know as happiness." Is there not a sense in which this exactly corresponds to the Spinozist account of joy? Deleuze says that "the *conatus* is the effort to experience joy, to increase the power of acting, to imagine and find that which is a cause of joy, which maintains and furthers this cause" (Deleuze 1981, 101). Joy is increase of the power of acting through union with that which increases our understanding. Perhaps the greatest example of this is the experience of love, in which one enters another world through contact with another body. But this conception is probably more Leibnizian than Spinozist, as this other world is monadic, self-contained, structured very differently from our own. The beloved gains the power to draw us into the 'depth' which they envelop only because they are *looking at us* from within the world that they inhabit. First, they express a world, but second, we are displaced from our own world, because they are seeing us from within theirs. "How can we gain access to a landscape that is no longer the one we see, but on the contrary the one in which we are seen?" (Deleuze 1964, 8).

Deleuze's interpretation of love is close to Jung's conception of the projection of the anima (CW 9ii, 13). Deleuze's development of a 'dialectic' of love is also his take on the Hegelian idea that the one who enters onto the path of desire will get more than he or she has bargained for. The encounter with the 'tribe' of girls causes Marcel's desire for possession to assume proportions that flow beyond the desire to capture the other as an image that serves to satisfy a pre-existent aim. "My desire for her was desire for her whole life": Marcel cannot help losing himself in the possible world that Albertine expresses, to the point that his own perspective is profoundly shaken, and he in turn must experience himself as a possible object in *her* world. It is the peculiar asymmetry in the relation to the other which gives rise to the jealousy which Deleuze claims is essential to love. The problem is that "the beloved's gestures, at the very moment they are addressed to us, still express that unknown world that excludes us. The beloved gives us signs of preference; but because these signs are the same as those that express worlds to which we do not belong, each preference by which we profit draws the image of a *possible world* in which others might be are or are preferred" (Deleuze 1964, 8). The opening up of the possible world in the loved other is simultaneously a joy and a torment, because, through entering it, the lover must encounter his or her own vanishing contingency. I am now a part of the loved one's world, more than he or she is part of mine, which can start to look miserable by comparison. Even though the loved other seems to be a 'sign' or a destiny ('it is meant to be'), as soon as she or he is taken as such, a cascade of 'what ifs' recoils back upon the lover. I have elicited this 'sign of preference,' but there must be others who can elicit it better than I. There is now a set of functions I must attend and fulfil in a strange world, with unknown inhabitants. The necessity of jealousy in love, says Deleuze, is 'the first law of love':

> Subjectively, jealousy is deeper than love, it contains love's truth. This is because jealousy goes further in the apprehension and interpretation of signs. It is the destination of love, its finality. Indeed, it is inevitable that the signs of a loved person, once we 'explicate' them, should be revealed as deceptive: addressed to us, applied to us, they nonetheless express worlds that exclude us and that the beloved will not and cannot make us know. Not by virtue of any particular ill will on the beloved's part, but of a deeper contradiction, which inheres in the nature of love and in the general situation of the beloved. (9)

But although the process of love will lead to an unexpected outcome for Marcel—jealousy, deception, and ultimately the realisation that what he sees in Albertine is an inverted image of himself—the process of love is more than a mere projection in the sense of the conscious desire for possession of a representative of an image. Even if it turns out that Marcel is ultimately repeating a virtual image that pre-exists Albertine herself, this is a genuinely *unconscious* repetition. There *is* an encounter with the Other, it is just that this Other will be one's unconscious. Love is a particular kind of encounter with the unconscious, through another person in an *unconscious* projection. It is a projection, but a projection of the unconscious by itself. In *Proust and Signs*, Deleuze explains the conceptual unity between difference and repetition in terms of love: "the unconscious, in love, is the separation of the two aspects of essence: difference and repetition ... Far from expressing the idea's immediate power, repetition testifies to the discrepancy here, an inadequation of consciousness and idea" (68). The process of love ultimately cannot 'express the idea' because of the unstable asymmetry between lover and loved. If there is an 'end' of the process of love, it is not to say that love withers away once the end has been attained. The point is that love is a very particular process: the meeting of the unconscious in external form. This process is finite, even if other, more elaborate processes come afterwards. For instance, Deleuze suggests that the amorous asymmetry can nevertheless be reflected to a higher power and thus controlled by retracing love back to the source of 'Initial Hermaphroditism' (80). Each sex is bisexual, in that it contains animus and anima; therefore love will be the encounter between two bisexuals, in each of which the male or female may be dominant respectively. Homosexuality and heterosexuality both emerge as selective, usually mutually exclusive choices from the 'primordial Image' of a divine hermaphrodite. In hermaphroditism, plants or snails cannot be fertilised 'except by other hermaphrodites' (80).[45]

Ultimately, however, "our only windows, our only doors, are entirely spiritual; there is no intersubjectivity except an artistic one. Only art gives us what we vainly sought from a friend, what we would have vainly expected from the beloved" (42). Deleuze cites a passage from the end of *In Search of Lost Time*, in which Proust returns to the image of the 'possible world' first opened up in the experience of love. "What sort of world was the one from which she was looking at me?" In love, the narrator felt as if he was looking through a telescope at a neighbouring planet, unable to imagine what interest the extraterrestrial intelligences that reside there might possibly have in him. It is only in art that a durable, subtle vessel can be created which preserves that "extension and potential multiplication of self which we know as happiness":

> Only by art can we emerge from ourselves, can we know what another sees of this universe that is not the same as ours and whose landscapes would have remained as unknown to us as those that might be on the moon. Thanks to art, instead of seeing a single world, our own, we see it multiply, and as many original artists as there are, so many worlds will we have at our disposal, more different from each other than those which revolve in infinite space, worlds which centuries after the

---

[45] Deleuze's remarks about the hermaphrodite that 'doubles each sex with itself' refer back to the esoteric notion of the hermaphrodite as 'double sex,' at the centre of Johann Malfatti's Tantric nature-philosophy, on which Deleuze wrote one of his first articles (see Kerslake 2007). Malfatti claimed the existence of an 'anima' and 'animus' in psychosexuality in his 1845 *Anarchy and Hierarchy of Knowledge*, almost a century before Jung took up the terms.

extinction of the fire from which their light first emanated, whether it is called Rembrandt or Vermeer, send us still their special rays. (Proust 1927, 254; partially cited in Deleuze 1964, 42; translation modified)

Only in the work of art does this microcosmic tendency of individuation succeed in its ultimate aim: "Art is the finality of the world, and the apprentice's unconscious destination" (Deleuze 1964, 50). Deleuze retains a teleological conception of individuation throughout his work of the 1960s, and the activity of the artist is always the highest form of individuation, not only because in artistic creation the individual achieves the most elaborate kind of self-differentiation, but also because the work of art gives individuality itself its most elaborate and solicitous expression. Creation is higher than the reception of art, but the latter is higher, more involuted, than love, which itself becomes further unfolded in art. Proust's hermetically sealed novel *In Search of Lost Time* is itself one of the dominant monads of Western culture. Complete interiorisation has been attained in the work of art, since it is the product of a pure manipulation of the 'free materials of nature' in the service of an Idea.

It is possible that Deleuze and Guattari's attack on the notion that it is possible to 'extrapolate' a transcendent object from the process of desire originates in Deleuze's Proustian analysis of the experience of love. Deleuze and Guattari's tendency to give primacy to desire therefore cannot be said to arise out of a radicalisation of the classical Freudian distinction between the 'object' and 'aim' of desire (SE 14, 122). For Freud, the fact that different types of sexual object can be substituted for one another in certain circumstances indicates that the object of the sexual drives is not essential to the satisfaction of the drives, which have their own distinct aims; the object and aim of desire are arbitrarily related. The Proustian background suggests that, by emphasising the productivity and creativity of desire, Deleuze cannot be understood to be reducing the role played by the object in the process of desire, no more than he can be understood as simply collapsing the distinction between subject and object of desire. In fact, he is precisely concerned with the *object* of desire. His point is that to desire a sexual object actualises a process whereby one's relation to the object leads into the *world* of the object. Desire is the subjective experience of entering the world of another in the protracted throes of a sexual relationship, which will in turn produce a reversal of the subject's initial desiring relation to his or her object. In fact, in *Proust and Signs*, Deleuze is less interested in desire in general than in the *process of love*—that is, falling in love, then the development of love in a relationship, and then, finally, the conclusion or end of love. For the early Deleuze, as we shall see, love is a *process* which reveals the truth of desire. Desire thus reaches its *end*—in the sense of completion and termination—through the process of love. And if this is right, it must be a mistake to discuss desire without reference to love.

Leibniz, Locke and the Uneasiness of Desire

Deleuze's remark to Claire Parnet that the notion of desire is best explained by referring to Proust raises more questions than it answers. In Proust, there is a 'dialectic of desire' quite different from the Lacanian one: desire dialectically unfolds into love and deception, finally finding its highest happiness in art. But this 'lunar' trajectory of the work of art leads desire away from the Earth altogether, and the achieved 'eternity' appears to put an end to the dialectic. However, this does not mean that there is nothing more to say about desire. On the contrary, the microcosmic destination of desire now (for us, the phenomenological observers) flows backwards into the whole field of human emotion, uncovering its hidden order. Returning to the concluding texts in Canguilhem's canon of the philosophy of desire allows us to discern what is fundamentally at stake in the 'choice' between the two dominant forms of desire. Canguilhem presents texts by Leibniz, Hegel (on the 'Negativity of Desire') and finally by Sartre which explore exactly the conception of desire to which Deleuze will later declare himself implacably opposed. The chapter ends with a passage from Sartre's *Being and Nothingness* to which Canguilhem gives the subtitle 'Desire as Lack and the Transcending of its Lack' [*Le désir comme manque et dépassement de son manque*] (Canguilhem 1954, 52). It is a critique of Spinoza's notion of the *conatus*, which Canguilhem has already presented. The explicit presentation of desire as lack (in relation to Sartre rather than Lacan) is striking and it suggests that Deleuze read this selection of texts by Canguilhem as a presentation of a dispute between two fundamental conceptions of desire: on the one hand, the positive conception which is inaugurated with Spinoza and ends with Proust, and on the other hand the negative conception inaugurated by Hegel and crystallised by Sartre.

Canguilhem makes the transition from Proust's notion of the proper object of amorous desire to negative notions of desire by presenting extracts from Leibniz's account of *l'inquiétude dans le désir* (disquiet in desire) in his critique of Locke, the *New Essays on Human Understanding*. Leibniz is quite taken with Locke's notion of the role of *uneasiness* in desire, and, in fact, Canguilhem's extracts really just relay Locke's concept of desire. Leibniz spends some time searching for appropriate translations of this English term, and settles on *inquiétude*, which he thinks comes closest. Locke says that "the uneasiness a man finds in himself upon the absence of anything, whose present enjoyment carries the idea of delight with it, is what we call *desire* ... The chief if not only spur to human industry and action, is uneasiness. For whatever good is proposed, if its absence carries no displeasure nor pain with it; if a man be easy and content without it, there is no desire of it" (Locke 1690, II.20.6; cited in Leibniz 1765, 163). The 'lowest degree of desire' (or 'velleity') is when the thought of the absence of the good thing causes no displeasure or unease. What determines the will to action, therefore, is not the good itself, but the unease: "This *uneasiness* we may call, as it is, desire, which is an *uneasiness* of the mind for want of some absent good" (Locke 1690: II.21.31). Or, in Leibniz's words, desire "is a disquiet of the mind caused by the lack [*manque*] of some absent good" (Leibniz 1765, 184). Thus in Locke's analysis of desire, we perhaps see the first glimmerings of the 'negativistic' conception of desire as lack. The Spinozist definition is not sufficient to define desire. It is not enough to say that in desire we are conceived to be 'determined, from any given affection, to do something' (E III, Definition 1). This does not distinguish desire from 'velleity.' Although Locke grants that velleity is 'the lowest degree of desire,' he says that 'there is next to none at all' in such 'faint wishes' (Locke 1690, II.20.6).[46] Mere determination to do something does not yet amount to *desire* proper. For desire to be present, the subject must also suffer from the thought of the absence of the desired object.

Locke, however, goes on to infer that, "pain and uneasiness being, by everyone, concluded, and felt, to be inconsistent with happiness [and] a little pain serving to mar all the pleasure we rejoiced in" we will necessarily be motivated towards the "removing of pain, as long as we have any left, as the first and necessary step towards happiness" (Locke 1690, II.21.36). Thus unease may be essential to desire, but the object of desire is to remove unease. Theophilus (as spokesman for Leibniz in the dialogue), however, counters this claim, and in this way seems to open the gate to the sanctification of negativity or lack in human desire which is taken up in the thought of Hegel, Sartre, and Lacan. "Far from such disquiet's being inconsistent with happiness," he argues, "I find that it is essential to the happiness of created beings; their happiness never consists in complete attainment, which would make them insensate and stupefied, but in continual and uninterrupted progress towards greater goods" (Leibniz 1765, 189). Such unease or disquiet is not just a stimulant to the will, it is essential to the kind of happiness that is proper to human

---

[46] Locke's description of velleity as 'faint wishes,' followed by his italicisation of *desire* in the next sentence, combined with the already cited passage from II.21.31, indicates that Locke thinks there is a difference in nature between velleity and desire.

beings. Happiness as the removal of unease is an aim fit only for beasts and the mentally exhausted. "Progress is inevitably accompanied by desire or at least by constant disquiet." So Leibniz intensifies Locke's claim about unease. Whereas Locke says that unease is essential to desire, Leibniz says that it is also essential to the satisfaction of desire. Leibniz's argument, however, is pitched at the ethical level rather than the empirical level of fact. Does Leibniz's text thus serve as the tipping point in the modern philosophy of desire, where 'lack' is not only found to be present in desire (through the uneasiness produced by the thought of the absence of the desired object), but indeed *must* be present in desire in order for desire itself to be redeemed from any tendencies it shows towards stupefaction? We seem to see desire in the process of becoming in itself a moral phenomenon in this text. Deleuze's words are already audible: "Desire: who, except priests, would want to call it 'lack'?" (Deleuze & Parnet 1977, 91). Leibniz does not seem to see that the introduction of lack into every corner of desire, and into its satisfaction as well, makes lack into something paradoxically excessive, introducing a 'primordial Discord' (Lacan 1949, 96) into the relationship of the human being to the world. Constant disquiet is part of a "healthy man's appetite ... unless it amounts to that discomfort which unsettles us and gives us a tormenting obsession with the idea of whatever it is that we are without" (Leibniz 1765, 189). For Sartre and especially Lacan, "a tormenting obsession with the idea of whatever it is that we are without" seems to be intrinsic to desire.

It is interesting, however, that, in his commentary on this passage in his 1980 lectures on Leibniz, Deleuze draws the opposite conclusion, and extracts Leibniz's thought from this fate. Deleuze first remarks that Locke's notion of unease (which he translates as *malaise*) is to be found 'in his best pages': "Locke tries to explain that it's the great principle of psychic life. You see that it's very interesting because this removes us from the banalities about the search for pleasure or for happiness" (Lectures on Leibniz, Third Lesson, 29 April 1980, 11). What Deleuze is interested in, however, is Leibniz's transformation of Locke's concept, which contains something other than an absolutisation of desire as lack. Deleuze points out that Leibniz's transformation of Locke's concept of desire first of all passes through his theory of minute unconscious perceptions. Leibniz contends that "there are hundreds of indications leading us to conclude that at every moment there is in us an infinity of perceptions, unaccompanied by awareness or reflection" (Leibniz 1765, 53). In the phenomenon of desire as unease, what we are seeing is the emergence of *unconscious* little perceptions, all struggling to incline the subject in a certain direction.

This unease of the living being, what is it? It's not at all the unhappiness of the living. Rather, even when [the living being] is immobile, when it has its conscious perceptions well framed, things are swarming [*ça fourmille*]: the minute perceptions and minute appetitions are investing the flowing perceptions [*perceptions fluentes*], ceaselessly moving in the flowing perceptions and flowing appetites. (53; translation modified)

For Leibniz, all living beings *express* the same world through their perceptual and affective capacities but with greater or lesser degrees of clarity and distinctness. The difference between beings is precisely in their degree of expression (Leibniz 1686–1687, 81). The tick's or worm's capacities for being affected are extremely limited, and so their minimal expression of the world shades off quickly into a great mass of obscurity. But a human being not only has a more sophisticated perceptual and affective apparatus, but also has the power of understanding. So when we are affected by something, we can not only perceive the affecting thing both clearly and distinctly, but we can even penetrate towards the forces that are behind the affections by tracing their causal background with our minds. Now, Leibniz argues that the more perfectly we express the distinct forces in the world, the less passive we become. Conversely, we can only be said to act, rather than be acted upon, when we express our essence clearly and distinctly—i.e. we know what we are doing (Leibniz 1686, 48). To speak, as human beings can, might be held to be something active, but to speak about something without really understanding it is precisely to be passive or 'acted on' (by received ideas, or ideas that are 'in the air' because of some nebulous trend). Insofar as human beings have understanding, they tend towards activity, and thus towards a more perfect expression of the world of which they are part.

But whence, then, comes the unease that accompanies desire? In the passage on unease in the *New Essays*, Theophilus tells his Lockean opponent that this constant disquiet "does not amount to discomfort, but is restricted to the elements or rudiments of suffering, which we cannot be aware of in themselves" (Leibniz 1765, 189). But what are these unconscious 'elements of suffering'? Is it because these minute perceptions are obscure and confused that we feel an unease stirring us from the depths the unconscious? Dizziness, swooning, and dying provide the models of unconscious perception to which Leibniz most often appeals. Is unease the result of the obscure and confused roaring of the ensemble of unconscious perceptions? Not at all. In Leibniz, we live in the best of all possible worlds, and so the unconscious perceptions which seek to be heard in the state of disquiet in fact all tend towards *one* aim: the perfect expression of our true nature. "So, if there is a God, and

Leibniz is persuaded that God exists, this 'uneasiness' is so little a kind of unhappiness that it is just the same as the tendency to develop maximum perception" (Deleuze, third Leibniz lecture, 11). The idea that we live in the best of all possible worlds is one of Leibniz's most fundamental metaphysical doctrines. Before the dawn of the world, God faces an eternal set of logically possible series, from which he must select a subset of series that are not only possible (non-self-contradictory) but compossible—compatible with *each other*. The ultimate criterion for his selection is the notion of the best of all possible worlds. When he analyses what 'the best' or 'most perfect' might mean, he states that it is "that combination of things ... by which the greatest possible number of things exists" (Russell 1900, 295; cf. Leibniz 1697, 151). The most perfect, or completely determined, world will be the world which has the greatest quantity of qualitative complexity while simultaneously having the minimum discontinuities. Now, obviously the unease of desire will be unhappy if it is passive, as this involves a loss of perfection. But there is nothing unhappy about the unease that is present in active desire. The disquiet that accompanies active desire is a part of increasing perfection. Disquiet is an aspect of joy! There is nothing, therefore, in Leibniz's transformation of Locke's theory of unease which necessarily leads towards the conception of desire as lack.

Hegel and the Negativity of Desire

The penultimate extract in Canguilhem's selection of texts from the philosophy of desire is from Jean Hyppolite's *Genesis and Structure of Hegel's Phenomenology of Spirit* (Hyppolite 1946, 160, 162–164; with omissions), which Canguilhem subtitles 'The Negativity of Desire according to Hegel' (Canguilhem 1952, 50). It concerns Hegel's genesis of the concept of desire from the concept of self-consciousness. The first form that self-consciousness takes is '*Desire* in general' (Hegel 1807, 105). At this stage of the *Phenomenology*, Hegel has arrived at a very general notion of self-consciousness; through the various preceding epistemological dialectics he has demonstrated that all knowing must involve the implicit appeal to normative criteria which contain the *rules* for knowing. Consciousness is thus implicitly self-conscious because acts of conscious cognition implicitly appeal to criteria which permit us to know that we are knowing, think that we are thinking, etc. But if all consciousness involves self-consciousness, then our apparently intentional directedness towards the world must always refer back to ourselves. The movement out towards otherness always requires a circular 'return to ourselves.' Thus in its most general sense, "self-consciousness is the reflection out of the being of the world of sense and perception, and is essentially the return from *otherness*. As self-consciousness, it is movement" (105). Now, what is the most elementary form that this might take? Self-consciousness implies that any object will always be mediated through me. In other words, at the most general level, the other is always *for* me. But what would this minimal conception look like if it was put into practice? Hegel suggests that it would follow that all appearances would be taken as just *means*—if the other is *for me*, then the other is just a means for my own self-realisation. "Certain of the nothingness of the other, [self-consciousness] explicitly affirms that this nothingness is *for it* the truth of the other" (Hegel 1807, 109 para. 174). If things are destined only for me, however, they nevertheless do really exist 'out there': if I wish to *satisfy myself*, I am forced to do it through an other. What is this form of relation to the world, says Hegel, other than *desire*? Desire is the most minimal form of self-consciousness, because it is a 'return to self' through the other. As Hyppolite puts it, "the end point of desire is not, as one might think superficially, the sensuous object—that is only the means—but the unity of the I with itself" (Hyppolite 1946, 160). If I understand the world solely through the lens of desire, I take myself to be faced with a world that is *for* me, but is nevertheless not immediately identical with me. In desire, I am always returning to myself through my enjoyment of others.

We have the pure form of desire, but now we must see what it would be like if this relation to the world were fully put into practice. The protagonist of such a worldview gets more than he bargains for, and thus begins the dialectic of desire which leads to the master/slave dialectic. In a first moment, I realise that my attempts to realise my desire are in fact conditional on the contingent features of the object of desire (Hegel 1807, 109 para. 175). Its presence or absence, its scarcity or availability, its adequacy in fulfilling my desire, are all out of my hands. And when I have satisfied one desire, another one appears. Although the pure form of desire first appeared to be a kind of sovereign relation to the world, I now find myself stuck on a wheel of desires and, rather than being a free, desiring creature, I am becoming a slave to my desires. I can never overcome my own dependence on my desired objects, and the sheer fact of my continual dependence on them produces a new form of otherness. It turns out that the sovereign subject of desire *cannot* satisfy himself after all. He becomes the loneliest being in the world; his accursed objects of desire stare back dumbly at him, forever separate, now negating *him*. How then can I find myself in the other, if I am so alienated from it? There is one remaining possibility—a ridiculously long shot, but still possible. What if there was an other, something that really was other, yet was not thereby permanently separated from me, but which *negated itself for me*. That *would* satisfy me! The only truly satisfying object of desire would be one that freely *gave itself* to the desiring subject. "On account of the independence of the object ... [desire] can achieve satisfaction only when the object itself effects the negation within itself" (109 para. 175). With this dream of the realisation of desire, we seem to enter a fantasy paradise, where trees bow down to present their fruits to the desiring subject, where animals bend their necks to be slaughtered. Has the desiring subject just retreated into a megalomaniacal, introverted fantasy? Has desire gone mad? Perhaps it has; there is nothing in the text to say that it has not. But Hegel implies that, by retreating into the farthest recesses of this introverted fantasy, by retreating into a radical interiority, the subject comes across the internal doorway that will lead out of itself once more. Addled with this fantasy, dragging itself through a landscape of dumb, mocking objects, the subject chances upon a strange sight. It is another addled maniac, bloated with food and drink, looking extremely unwell. The subject gazes at this uncanny sight, an obvious reflection of how he feels. And as he gazes in puzzled fascination, he witnesses a halo appear around the head of this apparition, darkening its visage. *This is the oasis*, he mutters to himself, awestruck and slightly repelled. For as the creature's face grows dark, he looks into its eyes. Here perhaps we encounter the meaning of that bloodshot fragment, 'Man, that Night': "we see [a] Night when we look a human being in the eye, looking into a Night that turns terrifying; it is the Night of the World that rises up before us" (Hegel 1805–1806, 87). We are present at the birth of Spirit (Hegel 1807, 110 para. 177), or 'social subjectivity' as Hegel's commentators now call it, as if wishing to conceal the weird manner of its birth. The goal of desire has been found: when the object of desire is *another* desiring consciousness, that other precisely possesses the potential to 'negate itself' freely before the subject, insofar as it can *acknowledge* it. "Self-consciousness exists in and for itself when, and by the fact that, it so exists for another; that is, it exists only in being acknowledged" (111 para. 178).

But of course this is only the beginning. The very moment when desire glimpses the possibility of satisfaction will turn out to be the beginning of a new movement, and will lead the subject away from 'desire,' properly speaking, towards an unanticipated struggle with this other. Because the arrival at the possibility of a self-negating other brings with it the implication that the subject must itself acknowledge that the other is looking at *him* from a precisely mirrored perspective, *he* will want the same from him. "A self-consciousness exists *for a self-consciousness*. Only so is it in fact self-consciousness; for only in this way does the unity of itself in its otherness become explicit for it" (111 para. 178). What began as an apparently sovereign self-consciousness desire thus culminates in a doubling of self-consciousness which changes everything: *two* self-consciousnesses now face each other, both wanting to be recognised. Hyppolite points out that, in Hegel's early writings, the possibility of mutual recognition is presented immediately in the form of *love*. "It would have been possible," notes Hyppolite, for Hegel "to present the duality of self-consciousnesses and their unity in the element of life as the dialectic of love … Love is the miracle through which two become one without, however, completely suppressing the duality" (Hyppolite 1946, 164; not cited in Canguilhem). But in the *Phenomenology* Hegel takes a different path. What happens next is the master-slave dialectic, which becomes the arena in which a new contradiction will now be played out: both self-consciousnesses will be caught up in the impossible task of getting *each other*, as *free*, to let themselves be *dominated*. Hyppolite concludes that "Desire is less the desire that characterises love than that of one desiring consciousness for the virile recognition of another desiring consciousness" (Hyppolite 1946, 164; Canguilhem 1954, 52).

Deleuze's exposition of Proust's reflections on love can be read as a critique of this interpretation of the dialectic of desire. Does the internal logic of desire necessarily lead into a 'virile' struggle for recognition? For Deleuze, the early Hegel was right: the internal logic of desire *does* lead towards love. He would disagree, however, with the early Hegel's suggestion that love is the achievement of mutual recognition; in fact, although love is the first real encounter with an other, it does not lead towards mutual recognition, but towards increasing jealousy and deception. If love manages to overcome this fate, it is not because of a final attainment of intersubjectivity. "Love, more lucid, makes it a principle to renounce all communication" (Deleuze 1964, 42). As individuals, we are ultimately monads, unconsciously repeating patterns that only gradually become conscious over the course of individuation. Love is the privileged and uncircumventable event in which one encounters one's own unconscious embodied in an external object.

In *Proust and Signs*, Deleuze suggests that mutual recognition or inter-subjectivity is not finally attainable through friendship, love, or any directly social relationship. The only way for an *individual* to reach that "potential multiplication of self which we know as happiness" is through the creation and experience of art. In fact, as it turns out, the final achievement of mutual recognition in Hegel's *Phenomenology* is not 'communicative' in any socially normative sense either. Mutual recognition only finally becomes realisable in a mutual act of forgiveness, in the wake of injury. Two subjects mutually recognise each other as the same because they acknowledge that they are *both* finite, sinning souls, with their own particular flaws. They are "purified into a unity in which there is no longer in them any existence devoid of self ... But they are different; and the difference is absolute because it is set in this element of the pure Notion" (Hegel 1807, 408 para. 671). But whereas, for Hegel, desire first unfolds in virility and ends in forgiveness, for Deleuze, desire unfolds in love and ends, somehow, in art. Ultimately, "our only windows, our only doors, are entirely spiritual; there is no intersubjectivity except an artistic one" (Deleuze 1964, 42).

As in Hegel's *Phenomenology*, Deleuze does not stipulate what the 'end' of intersubjective desire *should* look like. For Hegel, forgiveness is not a question of ethics (as Kierkegaard also saw, the purpose of ethics is to keep the subject striving towards the good, so ethics cannot acknowledge forgiveness, which in both Kierkegaard and Hegel becomes an affair for religion[47]). For Deleuze, although "the only intersubjectivity is an artistic one," this is not an ethical claim; it is just the result of Deleuze's version of dialectical formation or *Bildung*: 'apprenticeship.' If Hegel's *Phenomenology* is the "Science of the *experience* which consciousness goes through" (Hegel 1807, 21), for Deleuze, *In Search of Lost Time* is something similar: "an experience of signs that mobilizes the involuntary and the unconscious: whence the Search as interpretation" (Deleuze 1964, xi). At each stage, we get more than we bargained for, and the progression "proceeds for us, as it were, behind the back of consciousness" (Hegel 1807, 56). "Disappointment is a fundamental moment of the search or of apprenticeship: in each realm of signs, we are disappointed when the object does not give us the secret we were expecting" (Deleuze 1964, 34). But whereas, for Hegel, the series of disappointments on the 'highway of despair' (Hegel 1807, 49) all ultimately move towards a reconciliation of subject and object in the Absolute, Deleuze's apprenticeship concerns the increasing 'interiorisation of difference' in the subject. "On each line of apprenticeship, the hero undergoes an analogous experience, at various moments: *for the disappointment of the object, he attempts to find a subjective compensation*" (49). *In Search of Lost Time* is not about reconciliation with the world, or about the 'recollection' [*Erinnerung*] of the development of the shapes of consciousness in a common world history (cf. Hegel 1807, 7 para. 13). The 'return to self' which it depicts is a voyage through time: time is lost and then finally regained through the 'interiorisation of difference.'

---

[47] Hegel's account of forgiveness is the last section in the part of the book that deals with Spirit; after this passage begins the third and final part, on religion. If forgiveness is the realisation of mutual recognition ('The I that is a We and the We that is an I'; Hegel 1807, 110, para. 177), it is also the transition from Spirit to religion.

In Canguilhem's final text, from Sartre's *Being and Nothingness*, desire as lack is explicitly opposed to the Spinozist conception of desire. The Hegelian argument about the relationship between desire and negativity is pared down to its essence in Sartre's text. Analysis of the text shows, however, that it would be a mistake to treat Sartre's critique of Spinoza's notion of desire as a final showdown between desire as negation and desire as difference. Rather, in the light of the affinities we have discovered between Spinozist and Leibnizian desire, it is Sartre's own formulation that is exposed as an empty abstraction. The Sartrean version of negative desire, as fundamental, ontological lack, is opposed to desire in the form of difference more precisely insofar as it omits the fundamentally *temporal* basis of all differentiation and desire.

Sartre and Desire as Lack

The *Bildung* or 'formation' of desire according to Deleuze thus proceeds through love, to memory, and then finally to art. There are structural similarities with Hegelian *Bildung*, but the paths taken are completely different. Let us now complete our investigation into the philosophy of desire by turning finally to the last extract in Canguilhem's volume, which explicitly concerns Deleuze's anathema: desire as lack. Canguilhem cites a passage from Sartre's *Being and Nothingness*, which he entitles 'Desire as lack and the transcending of its lack' (Canguilhem 1952, 52; cf. Sartre 1943, 87–88, with omissions). Perhaps if we expound this passage, we will be able to see more clearly what is at stake in Deleuze's attack on the conception of desire as lack. Certainly, Sartre's explicit presentation of desire as lack in this passage suggests that Deleuze and Guattari's real target in their critique might be Sartre rather than Lacan. Even though Deleuze seems generally well-disposed to Sartre (in a eulogy written in 1964, he announces that "he was my master [*maître*]"; Deleuze 2002, 77, translation modified), perhaps he sees something pernicious in Sartre's doctrine of desire as lack, which he takes to have filtered into—and poisoned—Lacanian psychoanalysis. It also seems important that this very passage is presented by Sartre as a critique of Spinoza's theory of desire, which we saw that Canguilhem presented at the beginning of his selection. All this provides perfect conditions for the staging of a confrontation between Deleuze's affirmation of the positivity of desire in Spinoza, and the conception of desire as lack and negativity in philosophers ultimately influenced by Hegel's conception of desire.

The passage begins with an announcement that "the existence of desire as a human fact is sufficient to prove that human reality is a lack." Unlike Hegel's dialectical generation of the concept of desire and its internal consequences, Sartre situates the notion of lack in ontology and proceeds directly to a discussion of the empirical fact of desire, which is presented as a mere example. Sartre's claim about desire is thus directly rooted in the eponymous dualism that is the basis of *Being and Nothingness*. On the one hand, consciousness is always implicitly self-conscious and therefore must be taken as fundamentally *for-itself*. In effect, Sartre radicalises Hegel's claim in the *Phenomenology of Spirit* about the relation between consciousness and transcendence. Hegel says that consciousness is implicitly self-conscious because acts of conscious cognition implicitly appeal to criteria which allow us to know that we are knowing, think that we are thinking, etc.; "hence," Hegel says, "it is something that goes beyond limits, and since these limits are its own, it is something that goes beyond itself" (Hegel 1807, 51). Sartre effectively infers that this means that consciousness *is* only as *negativity*; 'being for-itself' is a pure 'lack of being' [*manque d'être*] (Sartre 1943, 85).[48] On the other hand, there is the world of non-conscious objects or physical states, in and for which there is no transcendence: this is being *in-itself*. In this sense, being is pure immanence, it 'is what it is,' as opposed to transcendence, which 'is what it is not and is not what it is.' In his argument about desire, Sartre is simply performing a classification of desire under the category of being for-itself, or pure negativity or lack. His argument takes the form of a *reductio*: "how can we explain desire if we insist on viewing it as a psychic *state*, that is, as a being whose nature is to be what it is? A being which is what it is, to the degree that it is considered as being what it is, summons nothing to itself in order to complete itself" (Sartre 1943, 87). Nor can desire be a '*conatus* conceived in the manner of a physical force' for the same reason. Sartre indicates that he has Spinoza's conception of *conatus* in mind when he says that "the *conatus* as *producer* of states cannot be identified with desire as the *appeal* from a state" (87); as we saw, for Spinoza, desire is man's essence, "insofar as it is conceived to be determined, from any given affection, to do something" (EIII, Definitions of the Affects, I). Sartre's objection to Spinoza is that his conception of psychophysical parallelism (between Thought and Extension) is incoherent when it comes to desire. "If we suppose an exact correspondence between the mental and the physiological, this correspondence can be established only on the basis of ontological identity, as Spinoza has seen." But the problem is that "thirst

---

[48] "Human reality by which lack appears in the world must itself be a lack. For lack can come into being only through lack; the in-itself cannot be the occasion of lack in the in-itself. In other words, in order for being to be lacking or lacked, it is necessary that a being make itself its own lack; only a being which lacks can surpass toward the lack" (Sartre 1943, 87; not cited in Canguilhem).

as an organic phenomenon, as 'physiological' need of water, does not exist"; *we* take ourselves as thirsty, but in the body there is just a series of positive phenomena, such as a coagulation of the blood. *Conatus* as extension will just be a physical state, while as thought it will involve something qualitatively different: the presence of a transcendence, the desire to leave one state to arrive at another. Thus either there is no ontological identity, or *conatus* is just physical and there can be no awareness of desire for the organism involved. But we know that desire exists (Sartre has started with the premise that it is a 'human fact'); therefore desire can only appear in the form of an ontological contradiction, a 'lack in being' (Sartre 1943, 88). This must not be taken to mean that desiring beings have an object-sized lack built into them; that would be to reinstall desire in being-in-itself. No, desire "is haunted in its inmost being by the being of which it is desire. Thus it bears witness to the existence of lack in the being of human reality."

How might Deleuze, all texts considered, defend Spinoza's theory of desire from Sartre's attack? The first thing to note is that, although Deleuze is often taken to be a Spinozist, his historical-philosophical studies of Spinoza contain many claims that are not repeated in the books that were 'written in his own name' (Deleuze 1968, xv), such as *Difference and Repetition*. That book does not even mention Spinoza's *conatus*. Deleuze, as we have suggested, is much more Leibnizian in his concerns (individuation, contingency, possible worlds, theodicy, the philosophically baroque, are the themes shared by Leibniz and Deleuze).[49] To turn more specifically to Deleuze's possible response to Sartre's critique of the Spinozist *conatus*, we might begin by conceding that Sartre has a point. From everything that we have seen about the importance of the synthesis of time for Deleuze's own philosophy, it follows that Deleuze would not have wanted to defend the psycho-physical parallelism that appears in

---

[49] In *What is Philosophy?*, Spinoza is called 'the Christ of philosophers,' because he manifested, for one moment only, 'the possibility of the impossible': a pure 'plane of immanence in which thought was adequate to being' (Deleuze & Guattari 1991, 60). But, after Kant, such a revelation becomes impossible once more. *Deus* is unfortunately dead, or at least has suffered a 'speculative death' (Deleuze 1968, 87). Deleuze admits this when he says that Kant's Copernican revolution, in which philosophies of Being and Substance are overthrown and we cast ourselves into an endless temporal becoming, must be taken up and pursued as far as it will go (Deleuze & Guattari 1991, 40). "Substance must itself be said *of* the modes and only *of* the modes. Such a condition can be satisfied only at the price of a more general categorical reversal according to which being is said of becoming, identity of that which is different, the one of the multiple, etc." (40). Although it might superficially seem as if this 'reversal' is a matter of flipping Spinoza over on his head, any closer inspection would show that what is involved is extremely complex, and would involve the elaboration of the entire complex passage through Kant, Fichte, Schelling, Hegel, Kierkegaard, Nietzsche, Bergson, Heidegger, to Deleuze himself.

Spinoza's philosophy. The *conatus* as quantitative physical force could not be identical in form to the *conatus* as experienced in cognition.

Bergson would have said the same; the nature of duration excludes the possibility of psycho-physical parallelism as Spinoza conceives of it. Bergson, however, did not have a philosophy of desire, so that comparison is of limited use. But Deleuze's philosophy of desire is built upon a Bergsonian framework, and this does already suggest ways in which Sartre's conclusion that desire is in itself lack can be avoided. His conclusion does not follow from his critique of psycho-physical parallelism, because his notion of a dualism between nothingness and being is too abstract. For Bergson and Deleuze, it is temporality that distinguishes us from 'being-in-itself,' not simply negation. And temporality on the Bergsonian model is not structured through negation, but by the particular form of heterogeneous differentiation. Bergson develops a theory of the past that unfolds, again in an extra-logical form, behind the thrust of duration. The ongoing temporal syntheses made by the finite agent are more than mere 'nothingness,' even if they do not 'exist' in the way physical actuality exists. For Deleuze (following Jung), the process of individuation is fundamentally durational and intensive, and this implies ordeals or encounters with 'singular points' whose ideality or virtuality does not make them any less binding on the actions of agents in the process of individuation.

In Deleuze's version of Proust's 'apprenticeship,' each phase of the process of individuation corresponds to a particular type of synthesis of time. At the beginning, there is the 'wasted time' of wandering around in various social milieus trying to find one's place. But then there is the experience of love, whose happiness is retrospectively understood to exist in its promise. "In love, the truth always comes too late. Love's time is a lost time because the sign develops only to the degree that the self corresponding to its meaning disappears" (Deleuze 1964, 87). With the end of love, one becomes lost in reminiscence, as the truth of love is the revelation of one's determination by one's past loves. "An original difference presides over our loves. Perhaps this is the image of the Mother—or that of the Father for a woman, for Mlle Vinteuil. More profoundly, it is a remote image beyond our experience, a Theme that transcends us, a kind of archetype" (67). But even if the governing 'primordial image' (68) is not a personal image, as it is with Freud, and is an impersonal archetype, as Jung claims, this encounter with the past is still achieved in the mode of reminiscence. With experiences such as that of the madeleine, however, the structure of time itself is revealed, thirdly, to be more complex than the model of reminiscence allows. With the surrender to 'involuntary memory,' one encounters the 'very being of the past in itself' (61), and one realises that what is most fascinating about the past is what has in fact *never been present*; Deleuze here goes beyond both Freud and Jung towards a view that is distinctively his own.

"Lastly, the signs of art define time regained: an absolute primordial time, a veritable eternity that unites sign and meaning" (87). Deleuze appears to be totally unashamed to say that art genuinely does offer a glimpse of eternity, the preservation of lost time. In art, essence itself is 'incarnated in substance' which are "ductile, so kneaded and refined that they become entirely spiritual; they are of course colour for the painter, like Vermeer's yellow, sound for the musician, words for the writer" (47). It is through such 'free substances' that archetypal forms can finally shake off their historical and temporal relations and achieve an expression which is eternal. The formal archetype only discovers an adequate expression in the 'free materials' of nature. "The real theme of a work is therefore not the subject the words designate, but the unconscious themes, the involuntary archetypes in which the words, but also the colours and sounds, assume their meaning and their life" (47). In his work on Kant's *Critique of Judgment* (cf. Deleuze 1963), Deleuze develops this account of the synthesis of archetype and free substance as a theory of symbolism. Kant's aesthetics makes possible a differentiation between the experience of symbols in the unconscious and the creation of artistic symbolism which is not developed in *Proust and Signs*.

Conclusion

After the discussion of desire in *Proust and Signs*, the next time Deleuze refers to the concept is in his brief discussion, mainly in footnotes, in *Difference and Repetition*. Freud is right, he says; "the unconscious desires, and only desires" (Deleuze 1968, 106). Desire is the activity of the unconscious, and, it would appear, is the only activity of the unconscious. At first glance, it would appear that Deleuze is distinguishing himself from those other early psychoanalysts like Jung and Adler, who took individuation and the lust for power as the fundamental motives of unconscious thinking, superior in importance to sexual desire. But the rechristening of libido as 'desire' (without specifying that it be *sexual*) is one of Jung's first moves against Freud. Jung points out that, in classical times, the Latin word *libido* had the more general sense of 'passionate desire' (CW 4, 111), or simply 'desire' (CW 4, 125; CW 4, 123). If desire is to be the main concept for treating psychosexual development, then it should take on the features ascribed to it by Jung, who is in opposition to Freud (cf. Deleuze 1968, 317). For Jung, desire is the positive response of the unconscious to 'problems' through the deployment of memory and imagination. The unconscious is not a mental domain filled with representations (memories and images of desired objects), but must first of all be referred back to the essential *problems* that punctuate the process of individuation and that provide the organising framework for one's actions. Jung proposes a threefold articulation of the appearances of the unconscious to the ego—first, it appears through projection as a 'shadow,' then the unconscious is embodied in the love object (anima and animus), and finally, in the terminus of absolute individuation, it appears as the unknown Self. Individuation terminates in a retrospective 'substantialisation' of unconscious productivity, so that a 'bottom up,' progressive conception of the movement of unconscious desire becomes possible. Jung sees the unconscious as the 'matrix' of the process of individuation, attempting to discover what really constitutes "the *positive* activity of the unconscious" (CW 8, 364), prior to its disturbance by repressions. (The repression of representations is a secondary phenomenon in the process of unconscious individuation, arising from a specific kind of conscious reaction to the 'problems' encountered in that process). Deleuze's understanding of desire in *Difference and Repetition* is explicitly indebted to Jung's conception. "Just as desire finds the principle of its difference from need in the virtual object, so it appears neither as a power of negation nor as an element of an opposition, but rather as a questioning, problematising and searching force which operates in a different domain than that of need and satisfaction" (Deleuze 1968, 106; translation modified).

This 'problematising' activity of the unconscious helps shed light on Deleuze and Guattari's critique of the Freudian and Lacanian 'paralogisms' of desire. Yes, desire involves the investment of objects, the fixation of the traces of their enjoyment in the memory, and the tendency to repeat those experiences. But that process of investment and fixation is an *intensive* process, and is thus a part of the ongoing process of individuation which starts in the womb. Freud's lack of interest in temporality means that he overlooks the fact that the process is intensive and ongoing, and is thus subject to the forward thrust of duration, with its discontinuities and thresholds. Desire develops in time, and is subject to the structures of time that govern finite living beings. If one keeps in mind these aspects of the individuation process, then it can no longer be assumed that desire is originally fixated to a complete, permanent object (whether that object is conceived of empirically or as something 'impossible,' as in Lacan), the lack of which thereafter motivates the process of desire. Desire is a productive and imaginative process, and unconscious repetition is a multiplicative, intensive process (i.e. it intrinsically involves difference, displacement, and phase-change). Rather than emanating from one object or event, the repetitions that unconsciously motivate desire bring with them the increments of previous repetitions, racketing up or lowering tension depending on whether or not a threshold has been crossed.

With its emphasis on archetypes and 'primordial images,' *Proust and Signs* remains indebted to Jungianism. But, although Jung's influence on Deleuze dates from early on in his career, Canguilhem's *Besoins et Tendances* reveals an alternative, philosophical architecture beneath Deleuze's philosophy of desire. Proust shows what the most interiorised Leibnizian monadology might look like when realised by finite beings, and demonstrates the internal relations between desire, love, and aesthetic creation. With this account of individuation in mind, a critical perspective on the theme of the 'negativity of desire' in Hegel and Sartre becomes possible. Love therefore could be said to remain the privileged form of desire in Deleuze's thought.

Abbreviations

CW *The Collected Works of C. G. Jung*. Edited by H. Read et al. Translated by R. F. C. Hull. 21 vols. Bollingen Series 20. New York and Princeton: Princeton University Press, 1953–1983.

E Spinoza. *Ethics*. Translated by E. Curley. London: Penguin, 1996. Standard referencing is used: 'E' for *Ethics*, followed by Part (1-5), then definition (D), axiom (A) or proposition (P) number.

SE *Standard Edition of the Complete Psychological Works of Sigmund Freud*. Edited by J. Strachey. 24 vols. London: Hogarth Press, 1958.

Bibliography:

Augustine. 1961. *Confessions*. Translated by R.S. Pine-Coffin. London: Penguin, 1961.
Canguilhem, G., ed. 1952. *Besoins et tendances*. Paris: Hachette, 1952.
Deleuze, G., ed. 1953. *Instincts et institutions*. Paris: Hachette, 1953.
———. 1963. 'The Idea of Genesis in Kant's Aesthetics.' Translated by D. W. Smith. *Angelaki* 5, no. 3 (2000), pp. 57-70.
———. 1964. *Proust and Signs*. Translated by R. Howard. London: Athlone, 2000.

———. 1968. *Difference and Repetition*. Translated by P. Patton. London: Athlone, 1994.
———. 1980. *Lectures on Leibniz*. Translated by C. Stivale. http://www.webdeleuze.com.
———. 1981. *Spinoza: Practical Philosophy*. Translated by R. Hurley. San Francisco: City Lights, 1988.
———. 1990. *Negotiations [Pourparlers]*. Translated by M. Joughin. New York: Columbia University Press, 1990.
———. 2002. *Desert Islands*. Translated by M. Taormina. New York: Semiotext(e), 2004.
Deleuze, G., and C. Parnet. 1977. *Dialogues*. Translated by H. Tomlinson and B. Habberjam. New York: Columbia University Press, 1987.
Deleuze, G., and F. Guattari. 1972. *Anti-Oedipus: Capitalism and Schizophrenia*. Translated by R. Hurley, M. Seem and H. R. Lane. Minneapolis: University of Minnesota Press, 1983.
———. 1991. *What is Philosophy?* Translated by G. Burchill and H. Tomlinson. London: Verso, 1994.
———. 1997. *L'Abécédaire de Gilles Deleuze*. Video. Directed by P.-A. Boutang. Paris: Editions de Montparnasse, 1997.
Freud, S. 1905. 'Three Essays on the Theory of Sexuality.' SE 7.
———. 1915. 'Instincts and their Vicissitudes.' SE 14.
Hegel, G. W. F. 1805–1806. *Hegel and the Human Spirit: A Translation of the Jena Lectures on the Philosophy of Spirit*. Translated by L. Rauch. Detroit: Wayne State University Press, 1983.
———. 1807. *Phenomenology of Spirit*. Translated by A. V. Miller. Oxford: Oxford University Press, 1993.
Holland, E. W. 1999. *Deleuze and Guattari's 'Anti-Oedipus': Introduction to Schizoanalysis*. London: Routledge, 1999.
Hyppolite, J. 1946. *Genesis and Structure of Hegel's 'Phenomenology of Spirit.'* Translated by S. Cherniak and J. Heckman .Evanston, IL: Northwestern University Press, 1974.
Jung, C. G. 1912. 'The Theory of Psychoanalysis.' CW 4.
———. 1927. 'Analytical Psychology and "Weltanschauung."' CW 8.
———. 1951. 'Aion: Researches into the Phenomenology of the Self.' CW 9.
Kerslake, C. 2007. *Deleuze and the Unconscious*. London: Continuum, 2007.
Lacan, J. 1966. 'Signification of the Phallus.' In *Écrits: A Selection*. Translated by B. Fink. London: Norton, 2004.
Leibniz, G. W. 1686. 'Discourse on Metaphysics.' In *Philosophical Essays*. Edited and translated by R. Ariew and D. Garber. Indianapolis, IN: Hackett, 1989.
———. 1686–1687. 'Letters to Arnauld.' In *Philosophical Writings*. Edited by G. H. R. Parkinson. London: J. M. Dent, 1972.
———. 1697. 'On the Ultimate Origination of Things.' In *Philosophical Essays*.

———. 1765. *New Essays on the Human Understanding*. Translated by P. Remnant and J. Bennett. Cambridge: Cambridge University Press, 1996.
Locke, John. 1690. *An Essay Concerning Human Understanding*. Edited by R. Woolhouse. London: Penguin Books, 1997.
Malfatti de Montereggio, J. 1845. *Études sur la mathèse ou anarchie et hiérarchie de la science*. Paris: Editions du Griffon d'Or, 1946.
Nogué, J. 1936. *La Signification du sensible*. Paris: Aubier, 1936.
Plato. 1974. *Republic*. Translated by D. Lee. London: Penguin, 1974.
Proust, M. 1919. *In Search of Lost Time, Vol. 2: In the Shadow of the Young Girls in Flower*. Translated by J. Grieve. London: Penguin, 2003.
———. 1927. *In Search of Lost Time, Vol. 6: Time Regained*. Translated by A. Mayor and T. Kilmartin. Revised by D. J. Enright. London: Vintage, 1991.
Russell, B. 1900. *The Philosophy of Leibniz*. London: Routledge and Kegan Paul, 1900.
Sartre, J.-P. 1943. *Being and Nothingness*. Translated by H. Barnes. London: Routledge, 1989.
Spinoza, B. de. 1677. *Ethics*. Translated by E. Curley. London: Penguin, 1996.

Anti-Oedipus: The Work of Resistance

Lyat Friedman

Oedipus is completely useless, except for tying off the unconscious on both sides.
(Deleuze & Guattari 1972, 81)

Oedipal desires are not at all repressed, nor do they have any reason to be ... Oedipal desires are the bait, the disfigured image by means of which repression catches desire in the trap.
(Ibid., 116)

Two threads of thought are woven together in Sigmund Freud's writing: The first, the Oedipal construction, setting off intense debates on and criticisms of the notions of subjectivity, identity, sexuality, and gender; the second, the defense mechanisms that are at work in the unconscious, instigating discussions on therapeutic techniques and notions such as resistance, projection, transference, and counter-transference.[50] The latter aspect runs from Freud's 1895 essay 'The Project for a Scientific Psychology' (SE 1) through Freud's papers on technique and his case histories. It is a thread that has remained in the background of most discussions of the Oedipal constitution of the psyche and which I hope to bring to the fore.

The first thread is one of content, be it Oedipal or sexual, with respect to Freud. It can also be found in other psychoanalytic writings, such as the good or bad breast as it is termed by Melanie Klein; fear of separation (or playing with threads), to use D. W. Winnicott's term; the unconscious in the radical sense of the word (i.e. the notion of the Other or lack of signification), as Jacques Lacan refers to it; femininity in Luce Irigaray's sense; or the dying mother in André Green's version.[51] The second thread is one of structure and constitution. It gives attention not to what is on the analysand's or the analyst's mind, but rather to the mechanisms of defense and to the resistances that are at work that the analysand is to become aware of and eventually dismiss. It is with these mechanisms that the analyst must work—resisting, projecting,

---

[50] The notions of projection, transference, and counter-transference will not be discussed in this paper, despite their importance.
[51] These are mere examples and do not pretend to be a comprehensive list.

introjecting, transferring, or counter-transferring, to name a few—that, when all goes well, give rise to the patient's experience of recollecting forgotten and repressed experiences or traumas.

These two threads of thought form the objectives of Freud's analysis. Freud claims, as early as 1910:

> There are now two aims in psycho-analytic technique: to save the physician effort and to give the patient the most unrestricted access to his [or her[52]] unconscious. As you know, our technique has undergone a fundamental transformation. At the time of the cathartic treatment what we aimed at was the elucidation of the symptoms; we then turned away from the symptoms and devoted ourselves instead to uncovering 'complexes' … now our work is aimed directly at finding out and overcoming the 'resistances,' and we can justifiably rely on the complexes coming to light without difficulty as soon as the resistances have been recognized and removed. (SE 11, 144)

And as late as 1937:

> It is familiar ground that the work of analysis aims at inducing the patient to give up the repressions (using the word in the widest sense) belonging to his [or her] early development and to replace them by reactions of a sort that would correspond to psychically mature condition. With this purpose in view he [or she] must be brought to recollect certain experiences and the affective impulses called up by them which he [or she] has for the time being forgotten. We know that his [or her] present symptoms and inhibitions are the consequences of repressions of this kind: thus they are a substitute for those things that he [or she] has forgotten. (SE 23, 257–258)

While both threads are important as such, I hope in this paper to weave these threads together and to show that Freud's notion of Oedipus can be understood as the means by which he brings to the fore his analysands' resistances in order to resist them. Then I expose the ego, the place of residence for consciousness and remembered experiences, as the major defense mechanism Freud constructs, and show that the id or the drives have a construction identical to that of the ego. In assaulting the id with the Oedipal theme, Freud removes the resistances of the patient and incorporates them into the ego. Finally, I present Gilles Deleuze and Félix Guattari's attempt to offer a different mechanism for the aching psyche by which therapy may conduct

---

[52] References to women have been added to all sexist quotes.

itself. That is, I hope to show how *Anti-Oedipus* is a text that works, one that resists the readers' oedipalized resistances and offers a non-oedipalizing mechanism by which one may undo the conformity and disciplinary unity Freud has offered.

Resisting Resistances

In 'The Interpretation of Dreams' Freud tells us not to pay attention to what the dreamer says but rather to listen to gaps produced by a second telling of the dream. That is, Freud advises us to listen to the betrayal of the dream's disguise. He says:

> In analyzing the dreams of my patients I sometimes put this assertion to the following test, which never fails me. If the first account given … is hard to follow I ask him [or her] to repeat it. In doing so he [or she] rarely uses the same words. But the parts of the dream which he [or she] describes in different terms are by that fact revealed to me as the weak spot in the dream's disguise. (SE 5, 512)

Freud is not interested in the content of the dream but in the different mechanisms of resistance that are revealed by the gaps in the two accounts. The fact that the same dream has varied accounts is understood by Freud to mean that the dream serves as a screen to an unconscious wish fulfillment, regardless of its content.

In a similar fashion Freud advises us not to listen too carefully to the patients' complaints or accounts of their symptoms. We must never write down, record, or try to remember what is said in analysis. Freud says:

> The technique, however, is a simple one … It consists simply in not directing one's notice to anything in particular and in maintaining the same 'evenly-suspended attention' (as I have called it) in the face of all that one hears. In this way we spare ourselves a strain on our attention which could not in any case be kept up for several hours daily, and we avoid a danger which is inseparable from the exercise of deliberate attention. For as soon as anyone deliberately concentrates his [or her] attention to a certain degree, he [or she] begins to select from the material before him [or her]. (SE 12, 111–112)

He adds: "The rule for the doctor may be thus expressed: 'He [or she] should withhold all conscious influences from his [or her] capacity to attend, and give himself [or herself] over completely to his [or her] 'unconscious memory'"

(SE 12, 112). The analyst must try not to remember what is said—strange advice from someone who remembers minute details of his conversations with his patients. Still, Freud adds, the analyst must unconsciously listen to the patient's unconscious—that is, listen to unconscious resistances and resist any interest in what is being said.

The analytic session must be conducted in a state of abstention. It is frustration, according to Freud, that causes the patient to be ill in the first place, and every decrease in his or her suffering can only weaken the force motivating the patient to heal. Thus, one must make sure that the patient's suffering does not end prematurely. It is the various resistances that bring about the suffering of a patient. By resisting the patient's resistances, by not listening to what he or she has to say, by not paying attention and refusing to support the patient emotionally, and by ignoring whatever troubles the patient, the analyst can posit certain resistances, produce a reaction of resistance from the patient in return, and, in so doing, detect the very resistances that the patient has used and that the analyst will reuse in his or her work.

Freud says, "People, faced in their lives by conflicts which they have found too difficult to solve, have taken flight into neurosis and in this way won an unmistakable, although in the long run too costly, gain from illness" (SE 11, 150). Neurosis is the set of resistances one has learned to use. It is the defense mechanism by which one inhabits or dwells in the world (to use a Heideggerian terminology) (Heidegger 1971, 145–161). Neurosis is the setting one produces in which he or she lives, a mechanism by which the difficulties of life or the internal complexities within oneself are ignored. However, "the gain from illness provided by the neurosis is nevertheless on the whole and in the end detrimental to individuals as well as to society: ... the energies which are to-day consumed in the production of neurotic symptoms serv[e] the purpose of a world of phantasy isolated from reality" (SE 11, 150). It is the role of the analyst to resist the symptoms of neurosis, to oppose its defense mechanism, to oblige the patient to face up to his or her resistances by preventing him or her from using such resistances. The resistance the analyst brings into therapy will compel patients "to be honest, confess to the [drives] that are at work in them, face the conflict, fight for what they want, or go without it" (150). The analyst must resist the escape that neurosis offers the patient.

Resistance, says Freud, is the patient's arsenal to be used in therapy. He or she repeats in therapy the resistances acquired in the past: the fixations, the unsuccessful positions, and the pathological symptoms. The analyst must uncover the resistance "which is never recognized by the patient, and acquaint him [or her] with it" (SE 12, 155). That is,

> One must allow the patient time to become more conversant with this resistance with which he [or she] has now become acquainted, to work through it, to overcome it, by continuing, in defiance of it, the analytic work … only when the resistance is at its height can the analyst, working in common with his [or her] patient, discover the repressed [drives] which are feeding the resistance; and it is this kind of experience which convinces the patient of the existence of and power of such [drives]. (155)

By resisting the resistances of a patient, a climax can be reached and the resistances overcome.

A hysteric, for example, substitutes satisfactions for his or her symptoms. He or she uses displacement as a defense mechanism. Thus the analyst has the task of identifying all the detours and of demanding the patient to give those up. The analyst must resist displacement by insisting on its impossibility. The phobic, on the other hand, avoids putting himself or herself in situations that cause anxiety. The analyst must therefore resist the phobic's avoidance. The agoraphobic, for example, must try to walk alone in the street and wrestle with his or her anxiety before his or her resistances are overcome in treatment. The obsessive provides a challenge by not bringing his or her resistances to the fore. Thus Freud advises us that the analyst should wait until the therapy itself becomes an obsessive activity, and then, with the use of counter-obsession, should forcefully defeat the obsession of the patient. The therapeutic technique is one of resistance; it resists the defense mechanisms by using them against themselves. The analyst becomes a mirror of resistances, refracting the unconscious defenses back to the analysand and forcing him or her to give them up and create different defenses.

So, without resistance, therapy cannot work. Such is the case, as Freud terms it, of homosexuality in a woman, like the 'beautiful and clever girl of eighteen, belonging to a family of good standing' (FH 145) whose parents sent her to seek Freud's assistance in 'curing' her symptoms and removing her inversion. After listening to the girl's tale, Freud concluded that the girl's sexual tendency was motivated by her mother's envy. In Freud's words:

> The mother herself still attached great value to the attentions and admiration of men. If, then the girl became homosexual and left the men to her mother (in other words, 'retired in favor of' her mother), she would remove something which had hitherto been partly responsible for her mother's dislike. (SE 18, 158)

Freud confirmed his interpretation and found reinforcement in the fact "that both parents behaved as if they understood their daughter's secret psychology. The mother was tolerant, as though she appreciated her daughter's 'retirement' as a favor for her; the father was furious, as though he realized the deliberate revenge against himself" (SE 18, 159). He then presented his interpretation to the girl, hoping to generate objection and resistance on her part. Freud says, "Once I expounded to her a specially important part of the theory, one touching her nearly" (SE 18, 162). To his surprise, however, "she replied in an inimitable tone, 'How very interesting,' as though she were a *grande dame* being taken over a museum and glancing through her lorgnon at objects to which she was completely indifferent" (162). She offered no resistance. She did not object or refuse his interpretation. Freud immediately concluded the therapy, though he recommended its continuation with a female therapist.[53] Freud concluded, "She was in fact a feminist; she felt it to be unjust that girls should not only enjoy the same freedom as boys, and rebelled against the lot of woman in general" (SE 18, 169). More importantly, Freud says, "the material impels us to conclude that it is rather a case of congenital homosexuality" (SE 18, 170)—i.e. the girl was an invert but she was not psychically ill. Without resistance, there is no therapy and, even, a kind of 'normality.' Without resistance, Freud could only conclude that the analysand was healthy, despite being a 'feminist.'

Producing Resistances

That resistance is essential to psychoanalysis is not surprising. As Jacques Derrida concludes, "There is no analytic position once resistance is not identifiable" (Derrida 1998, 32). But it is not merely an issue of identifying resistances. What is at stake here is the mechanism by which Freud produces resistance in his patients so as to identify it. In this sense, it is the first thread, the Oedipal thread, which provides Freud the means of conjuring up resistances. If Freud had interpreted the girl's behaviour in a different light, would he have been able to produce the 'desired' objections from her? Perhaps. Would a different interpretation imply a therapy that is not based on resistances? To

---

[53] Though Freud stresses the notion of transference I have not dealt with it here, despite its being an important mechanism in therapy (I fear it will take too a long detour). In this case, because Freud thought that the girl identified him with her father, or rather, because Freud identified his position as analogous to that of her father, the transference of her unconscious resistances from her father to him would not assist the therapy. Nonetheless, Freud concluded that the girl, despite being a feminist and homosexual, was psychically healthy.

answer that, allow me a plunge into the case of the Wolfman to examine the variety of interpretations that Freud offers to his reader.

Much has been said and written about the Wolfman (Abraham & Torok 1986). What is interesting, in this case, is the number of different kinds of interpretations Freud offered and the way in which various symptoms dissipated as he offered each interpretation. At first, Freud remarks, "The patient ... [was] for a long time unassailably entrenched behind an attitude of obliging apathy. He listened, understood, and remained unapproachable" (SE 17, 5) (after all, the Wolfman was obsessive). As the analysis progresses, we are first told that, with a single blow, he recalled his sister's sexual seduction: "His sister had taken hold of his penis and played with it, at the same time telling him incomprehensible stories about his Nanya" (15). Then Freud claims that "it was not he who had played the passive part toward his sister, but, on the contrary, he had been aggressive, had tried to see his sister undressed, had been rejected and punished" (15). Then Freud revises his claim (after the account of the dream) and informs us that, at puberty, the Wolfman tried to seduce his sister but was rejected, while at the age of three and a quarter his sister did seduce him. Then a new and more fantastic interpretation is given: that of the primal scene: At the age of a year and a half, while suffering from malaria, the Wolfman was brought into his parents' bedroom and when "he woke up, he witnessed a coitus a tergo (from behind), three times repeated; he was able to see his mother's genital as well as his father's organ" (38).

Freud, I think, is overwhelmed by this possibility, or perhaps by the impossible image he has given—if only one considers the position that the child should have been in so as to be able to watch the scene and recall every detail. Accepting the occurrence of the primal scene implies accepting an impossible experience. And Freud is indeed troubled. In a footnote he adds, "At the age of one and a half the child receives an impression to which he is unable to react adequately; he was only able to understand it and to be moved by it when the impression was revived in him at the age of four" (48). Freud reminds us over the next pages that phantasies from an earlier age are not necessarily true, that "these scenes from infancy are not reproduced during treatment as recollections, they are the products of construction" (55).[54] Then, Freud offers us a different interpretation, one that will "relieve us of many of our difficulties" (63). "Perhaps", Freud writes, "what the child observed was not copulation between his parents but copulation between animals, which he then displaced

---

[54] Freud rejects the claim that these scenes are 'phantasies not of the patient but the analyst himself' (SE 17, 57). He insists that the constructions made in analysis belong to the patients. Had Freud done so, the Oedipal theme he constantly brings into analysis would have been shattered and would no longer be used.

on to his parents ... The wolves in the dream were actually sheep-dogs and ... the boy was repeatedly taken to visit the flocks of sheep" (63).

I will not go further into the sexual scenes the boy was said to have witnessed and the various seductions tempting his tender mind. What is important here is that Freud realises that his interpretation is troubling and fantastic. Unable to accept his own interpretation, Freud resists himself. And while the Wolfman improves and his symptoms dissipate, resistance itself works in both directions: from analysand to analyst and from analyst back to analysand, and the readers. What troubles Freud in his writing is not the resistances the Wolfman has to offer—the effects of his interpretation are enough to convince him—but his own resistances and the resistances he seems to be anticipating from the reader. Freud, in writing his case, is working with the reader in the same manner he claims to be conducting his treatment.

The primal scene offered, the explicit sexual scene, is the means of producing resistance. The more scandalous the content of the interpretation, the more likely resistance will take place. As a reader of 'The Wolfman,' one cannot but reject out front Freud's interpretation, and so Freud refines his tale; he resists the reader's resistance. In rejecting the primal scene of the Wolfman's tale, Freud provides the reader in advance a more subtle version, an acceptable one, which becomes acceptable if only because the previous image was too outrageous, even to Freud himself. In producing resistance in the reader, Freud offers an alternative that is more tasteful and yet, in its essence, is not very different from the initial tale. That is, in Freud's eyes, the two scenarios— the Wolfman's act of watching dogs copulate and his claim that he saw his parents do so—are analogous, because the former is more likely, and the latter inconceivable.

Because we resist the primal scene, the scene of the dogs becomes a reasonable possibility. Had Freud initially interpreted the Wolfman's dream as a reconstruction of the scene of the dogs, the likely question of why such a scene should become so troubling to a young child would have been asked. And Freud does not ask it. Nor does he ask why primal scenes of sexual coitus, which are not supposed to be understood by such tender minds as the young Wolfman's, become so troubling. Freud understands the power of resistance and he also understands the mechanism by which an outrageous proposition serves to soften our resistance to a more subtle or reasonable one. Nonetheless, it is the resistance to the primal scene, to an impossible scene, and to a scene that cannot be understood, that does the work in convincing us to accept Freud's interpretation. That is, the Oedipal scene is a diversion for the reader, a fixation point for resistance, which, once it takes place, brings the reader into accepting Freud's analysis.

Unlike the Wolfman, the homosexual girl, who did not resist Freud's interpretation when she indifferently exclaimed, 'How very interesting,' was not scandalised by Freud. After all, she was a feminist and a lesbian and thus she was more extreme than Freud dared to think. His termination of the therapy was his own resistance, not hers. He resisted being told that women can find men unattractive—a thought more scandalous than a girl's 'retiring in favor of' her mother. To think in those terms demanded from him overcoming resistances he could not afford to face.

This may well explain the problem analysts may be facing in our post-Freudian society. To go into analysis and to discover that an earlier Oedipal scene is the cause of certain symptoms and anxieties I may have had can no longer do the job. Oedipus has been so well accepted and incorporated in the layperson's understanding and self-reflection, that it does not have the shocking effect it must have had in Freud's time. Further, these days one goes to analysis with an Oedipal expectation, seeking to discover some repressed event about one's parents. This expectation on the analysand's part removes the possibility of producing resistances in light of the analyst's interpretation. Expecting a primal scene of sorts undermines the therapeutic effect. Deleuze and Guattari say: "The subjects of psychoanalysis arrive already oedipalized, they demand it, they want more" (Deleuze & Guattari 1972, 121).

That the Oedipal theme overshadows Freud's works is not new, but the notion that the Oedipal theme is not a necessary theme to invoke in order to bring about resistances must be understood. Jacques Lacan's work and his insistence on the non-meaning and the Other as the theme of his work testifies to that effect. By resisting his patients' attempts to discover and reveal sexual desires or phantasies, by insisting that one cannot and does not know what is repressed, or what hidden meaning lies behind a chain of signifiers, Lacan produces the desired effect in his patients. Lacan's patients and readers resist the lack of meaning and the lack of significations they desired from him as an analyst. Lacan resists the demand of language and the demand of his patients to speak, and to speak Oedipally, by remaining silent. Lacan does so in all of his writings, when he makes statements such as, for example, "We will fail ... as long as we cling to the illusion that the signifier answers to the function of representing the signified, or better, that the signifier has to answer for its existence in the name of any signification whatever" (Lacan 1966, 150). He does so when he comments on the notion of sexuality by saying, "The reality of the unconscious is sexual reality—an untenable truth" (Lacan 1978, 150). Lacan exemplifies this in his interpretation of Poe's 'Purloined

Letter.'[55] It is not important what the content of the hidden letter is, nor the content of one's repressed memories, rather, it is the mechanism that resists signification that must be articulated. And Lacan illustrates the same point again in his discussion of Antigone, saying she goes beyond *Atè*, beyond the limits of language. "Antigone's position represents the radical limit that affirms the unique value of [Creon's] being without reference to any content... . The unique value involved is essentially that of language. Outside of language it is inconceivable" (Lacan 1992, 279). What is troubling to us in Antigone's image is the impossibility to give meaning and grasp her motivation. We resist by imposing our moral judgment in the attempt to discover what motivates Antigone's actions because we fail to understand her. That is, Lacan repeats over and over the necessity of the analyst to fail to provide meaning and significations,[56] and thus produce the desired resistance.

Gilles Deleuze and Félix Guattari's *Anti-Oedipus* produces resistance of a different kind. They do not insist on an Oedipal theme; in fact, they categorically reject it. Nor do they attempt to insist on the 'impossibility of meaning' as Lacan does. Instead, they offer the reader, as well as the analysand, the potential of becoming a machine. In objecting to Freud's Oedipus, like Freud and Lacan, they offer us an alternative set of signifiers which we as readers must resist, despite the excitement this possibility produces in us. What one finds so exciting and liberating in *Anti-Oedipus* is not the image of machine and of the body without organs or the contemplation of the desiring-production one imagines while reading the text, but rather that as one attempts to think of/resist oneself in mechanical terms, one discovers profound relief from the moral and constraining demand to become and to think of oneself in terms of the Oedipal construction.

The opening lines of *Anti-Oedipus* produce the same perplexity as Lacan's insistence on non-signification to an Oedipal audience, or Freud's insistence on a primal scene during his time:

> It [functions] everywhere, functioning smoothly at times, at other times in fits and starts. It breathes, it heats, its eats. It shits and fucks. What a mistake to have ever said the id. Everywhere it is machines— real ones not [metaphoric] ones: machines [of other machines] with all the necessary couplings and connections. (1972, 1)

---

[55] Muller & Richardson 1988.
[56] Unlike Jean-Luc Nancy's and Phillippe Lacoue-Labarthe's claim in *The Title of the Letter* (Nancy & Lacoue-Labarthe 1992), Lacan does not attempt to show the truth of the psychoanalytic system in the failure of the linguistic chain. Lacan, I think, is exposing and insisting on such failure because it is failure itself that produces resistances and allows the individual to rework the defense mechanism unconsciously.

There is, here, a play on words that does not come across in English: Id – it. Id, the very source of psychic energy, the agency of one's unconscious drives, that from which desires are formed, is a production machine. Irresistible! It produces in an Oedipal reader an image as powerful as the Oedipal primal scene.

Do Lacan, Deleuze, and Guattari resist Freud's Oedipus? They do and they do not. Their objection to the sexual interpretation rests on the acceptance of the mechanism of resistance. In offering a different content with which to create resistances, they show an appreciation of Freud's great 'discovery.' They resist the content Freud provides his patients while not resisting the work of resistance that can produce such contents. While Lacan provides us with an empty image by which to reorganize our defenses, Deleuze and Guattari provide us with a mechanical image (despite and because of their insistence that the machine/psyche is not an image[57]). Both images produce resistances and, in so doing, release us from the crippling bonds of a rather disturbing image.

Resisting Ego/Ids

> We recognize in human beings a mental organization which is interpolated between their sensory stimuli and the perception of their somatic needs on the one hand and their motor acts on the other, and which mediates between them a particular purpose. We call this organization their '*Ich*' ('ego'; literally the 'I').... . Besides this 'I,' we recognize another mental region, more extensive, more imposing and more obscure than the 'I,' and this we call the '*Es*' ('id'; literally, 'it'). (SE 20, 194–195)

Freud continues, "We suppose that the ego is the layer of the mental apparatus (of the id) which has been modified by the influences of the external world.... . The ego lies between reality and the id, which is what is truly mental" (194–195). The ego, so far, is an external layer mediating between the world and the id.

---

[57] While Deleuze and Guattari insist that the machine is not an image, an oedipalized reader cannot help, while reading the text, but imagine a machine. That is, before one is able to overcome the resistances the text produces, one must imagine oneself, while still retaining a self, to be like a machine. It is only after the oedipalized resistances are removed that one may attempt to become a machine, though I do not think that Deleuze and Guattari aim to shape the psyche of the reader. They are set to destroy the Oedipal defense mechanism, not to shape the reader in any way, as Freud has done.

Freud goes on:

> We assume that the forces which drive the mental apparatus into activity are produced in the bodily organs as an expression of the major somatic needs.... We give these bodily needs, in so far as they represent an instigation to mental activity, the name of '*Trieb*' [drives].... Well, then, these [drives] fill the id: all the energy in the id, as we may put it briefly, originates from them. Nor have the forces in the ego any other origin; they are derived from those of the id. (SE 20, 200)

The ego and the id are agencies containing psychic energy and are there to satisfy bodily need. The ego is an external layer enclosing the drives within and mediating the external world in the attempt to provide satisfaction to the drives which are the id. Id, on the other hand, is contained by ego and restricted by it. It too produces a kind of envelope from within, differentiating itself from the larger container, the ego.

How is such differentiation made possible, Freud asks, and responds, "if the [drives of] id's demands meet with no satisfaction, intolerable conditions arise" (SE 20, 200). When ego is unable to meet the demands of the drives, because the external situation does not lend it the opportunity to satisfy id, ego, in its attempt to preserve itself and avoid traumatic experience, "treats the danger [of the id] as if it was an external one; it makes an attempt at flight, draws back from this portion of the id and leaves it to its fate" (203). Ego, unable to satisfy its own drives, cuts these drives off from within itself, contains them, represses and isolates them to the degree that they are inaccessible as id.

In other words, ego and id are initially fields of energy seeking satisfaction. When the world does not provide satisfaction or proves to be a force more powerful—causing what Freud terms trauma[58]—ego reacts against itself and isolates from within itself the energy that has just been frustrated. In so doing, ego sets itself apart from id, from its drives, and uses much of its energy in attempting to keep the id, the drives, from overflowing into itself.

Further, the resistances ego imposes on the drives are the same resistances ego uses to isolate itself from the world. That is, ego uses resistances that form

---

[58] One must distinguish between two types of trauma. A primary trauma is the experience of a force penetrating the individual's (ego-id) energy field and is one in which the individual (ego-id) does not have the mechanism to defend itself; thus the experience is meaningless and cannot be understood. Secondary trauma is an experience that occurs after the ego has split itself from the id, and so the individual (ego) has the mechanism to defend itself and translate the experience into a meaningful event. The experience becomes traumatic if the meaning of the event is overwhelming to the ego and so ego represses the event and makes it unconscious. Here, Freud is discussing primary trauma, one in which the experience remains unknown and not understood.

ids which are the introjections of the resistances ego projects from itself onto the world. Ego isolates itself from the world and forms closures of defenses against the world and then turns against itself and forms smaller, isolated closures of its own drives within itself. The resistances ego exercises against the world and against itself, according to Freud, are identical.

Patients who seek Freud's advice are individuals with an ego that spends too much energy in its attempt to shut off id and contain the drives. Resistance, then, is ego's defense mechanism against itself and the world. In these individuals, it is the mechanism by which ego attempts to isolate the id unsuccessfully. Freud thus says, "Our therapeutic aim [is] to restore the ego, to free it from its restrictions, and to give it back the command over the id which it has lost owing to its early repression" (205). Freud will attempt to resist the resistances of the ego in its attempt to control the id and, in so doing, to break through the isolation of id from the ego and to allow ego to incorporate the energy back into itself. In so doing, ego rids itself of its repressions and allows the energy emitted from the id to reconnect with ego. The weaving of the drives back into ego produces the feeling of recollection and recalled memories. Freud says, "We have to seek out the repressions which have been set up and to urge ego to correct them with our help and to deal with conflict better than by an attempt at flight" (205).

In treatment, by resisting the resistances ego conveys, the analyst assists ego in re-forming itself as a whole. As Lacan notes, "the restitution of the subject's wholeness appears in the guise of a restoration of the past" (Lacan 1988, 14). The experiences the analysand recalls are, as Freud says, constructs that are the outcome of resistances to the Oedipal scene that Freud suggests so as to produce the resistances that ego imposes on id. That is, because Freud proposes a scene that must be resisted, the access through the resistances of ego is the very same resistance of ego to id and it provides the content by which ego incorporates the id into itself. In the initial isolation of id from ego, ego acts as though id is external to itself. Now, in treatment, by having the resistance refracted back onto itself, ego acts as though what is resisted, the Oedipal scene, is within id, which is integrated back into ego.

Thus Lacan is also right in noting that if the function of the ego is in isolating by resisting, then "in the end, the id and the ego amount to exactly the same thing" (16). Just as ego is isolated from the world, so is id isolated from ego—"The human ego, namely that set of defenses, of denials, of dams, of inhibitions, of fundamental fantasies which orient and direct the subject" (17). While resistance makes treatment possible, "everything which destroys the continuation of the work is resistance" (33), says Lacan. Ego is a set of defense mechanisms which resist the boundaries by which ego has isolated itself from the world and from the drives.

Is it possible "to dispose of a conflict between a [drive] and the ego, or of a pathological demand [of the drive] upon ego, permanently and definitively?" (SE 23, 224), Freud asks. And he replies:

> This is in general impossible, nor is it at all to be desired. No, we mean something else, something which may be roughly described as a 'taming' of the [drive].... . The [drive] is brought completely into the harmony of the ego, becomes accessible to all the influences of the other trends in the ego and no longer seeks to go its independent way to satisfaction. (225)

According to Freud, once resistances are removed, the drive finds its way back into the ego and dissolves its isolation. Recollecting constructed experiences, finding meaning by resisting the Oedipal tale, weaves the drive into a network of Oedipal details that, despite one's resistance to it, resonate and echo what is resisted. Because the drive has no content of its own, because the drive was isolated at an early age in at which ego had not yet acquired the mechanism by which the world made sense to it, the drives remain without content; thus, what is resisted in treatment serves as the material to which the drives attach themselves. In this process, forgotten memories become accessible to the analysand. These memories are what Freud terms psychic constructs.

That Deleuze and Guattari resist Freud by offering a different image, the image of the machine, is not surprising. But they are very clear. The machine is not an image or a metaphor. It is the real thing. They are resisting the resistances that transform 'being' into images of being in the world—they resist a 'world "picture."'[59] When we read *Anti-Oedipus*, however, we cannot help but produce an image which resists our imaginary capacities. The image of the machine, which we produce in resisting Deleuze and Guattari, is an image whose contents once weaved into the drives that can only shake the very foundation of ego and its powerful resistances. Deleuze and Guattari resist ego and its images.

Further, the resistance to ego is also a resistance to the imposed incorporation of id back into ego. Deleuze and Guattari offer us the mechanical schizo who has no ego. The schizo does not sever the isolation of the id or the drives. Instead,

---

[59] Heidegger says, "The fact that the world becomes picture at all is what distinguishes the essence of the modern age" (Heidegger 1977, 130). Modernity offers us a worldview, an image of the world and an image of ourselves viewing the image of the world. We can no longer detach ourselves from the representation of our selves.

the schizo dissolves the constraining shield of ego and sets free the isolated ids without reconnecting them into one whole. What Deleuze and Guattari resist is the imposing harmony Freud offers. They resist the construction of ego that is supposed to reflect the father's image and one which takes it upon itself to bring order into the house and discipline the psyche. "The schizo is the one who escapes all Oedipal, familial and personological references—I'll no longer say me. I'll no longer say daddy=mommy—and he [or she] keeps his [or her] word," say Deleuze and Guattari (1972, 361–362).

In Lacan's case, no image is offered, or rather, the image of nothing is offered. That is, Lacan offers the Real—that which has and cannot have an image. Lacan resists ego and resists the image of ego as a defense mechanism that resists the drives. In that sense, the effect of Lacan's resistances has an effect similar, though of a different kind, to Deleuze's and Guattari's work. These thinkers work to undo the bonds of Freud's ego to an over-oedipalized audience and readers. This explains the difficulty of reading Lacan. The reader is immersed in his or her inability to make sense of Lacan's texts, just as the reader of Deleuze and Guattari finds himself or herself mechanically and rhythmically in the text. Reading Lacan implies resisting the impossible. It implies that one cannot understand the text and is forced to work on his or her attempts to find Oedipal meanings. In so doing, Lacan's writings demand of the reader to find alternative ways to express one's drives. Reading Deleuze and Guattari implies becoming a reading machine. An Oedipal reader who attempts to find meaning in the machine offered in *Anti-Oedipus* is resisted by the text and is thus forced to divert his or her drives away from Oedipus and discover other means of expressing the ids. In this sense, Lacan, Deleuze, and Guattari produce in the reader a positive force and not merely a reactive one.

Freud's therapeutic mechanism is aimed at restricting the ids and placing them under the commanding harmony of the ego. It is a mechanism that uses a limiting force by not allowing the drives to express themselves. Deleuze and Guattari attempt in *Anti-Oedipus* to provide a positive force, one that can break through the limitations of ego and the family scene and set free the drives to express themselves without being restricted. Like Lacan, they demand the reader to stop the process of identification, as humans and as readers of their texts. *Anti-Oedipus* is a text that works—it works to allow the reader to overcome negative resistances and become a positive, creative, force.

Antigone's Moral Claims

In *Antigone's Claim*,[60] Judith Butler makes the important claim that one should not differentiate between the state and the family – as Hegel does in his contention that the family and the state are of the the same order and structure (Hegel 1807, 266) - and she argues that Antigone is not caught in dialectic relations of the family/nature struggle with man/state for recognition. Butler resists the outer layers of the defense mechanism: the family, represented this time as the drives; and the state, represented as ego. Like the analysand in a Freudian treatment who must overcome ego's resistances so as to penetrate the internal defenses of ego and dissolve the inner resistances of the id, here Antigone is understood to be the drives struggling to force their way out of the resistances of the ego. Antigone, Butler claims, should not be thought of as representing the family fighting the state; rather, she claims, Antigone is undermining both family and state, because there is no difference between the family and the state. Both institutions, the family and the state, function as repressive and disciplinary layers of ego.

Because Antigone resists both familial and state relations, she is, in Butler's eyes, cutting off the bloodline as the origin of kinship. She undoes, according to Butler, the fundamental and 'natural' structure that binds the family to society. She defies the symbolic order in a speech act and "upsets the vocabulary of kinship that is a precondition of the human, implicitly raising the question for us of what those preconditions really must be" (Butler 2000, 82). In appealing to kinship, Antigone refuses to reduce kinship to the family and performs what Butler terms radical kinship.

In reducing Antigone to an id struggling with ego, the family, and the state, Butler characterizes a perverted Oedipal family. Antigone's repetitions are understood, in this scheme, to be performative acts that depart from the symbolic order of the state/family/ego—i.e. Oedipal sexuality and gender practices. Every deed in the tragedy, Butler claims, is preceded by a speech act and Antigone's "words are repeated and their repeatability relies on the deviation that the repetition performs" (58). The resistances that Antigone's performance produces leads Butler to conclude that Antigone is resisting the incest taboo, the Oedipal construct. Antigone's performance challenges us to rethink radical kinship, Butler claims. She "does seem to deinstitute heterosexuality by refusing to do what is necessary to stay alive for Haemon, by refusing to become a mother and a wife, by scandalizing the public with her

---

[60] Much of Butler's work deals with the notion of performance and performablity; here I will only refer to her *Antigone's Claim: Kinship between Life and Death* (cited as Butler 2000).

wavering gender, by embracing death as her bridal chamber and identifying her tomb as a 'deep dug home'" (76). According to Butler, Antigone's performance serves to destroy the outer layers of resistances of state/family/ego and thus can set the drives loose and reconstruct her sexuality.

What Butler forgets, however, is that, in so doing, Antigone does not achieve relief and her drives are put to death in the process. She is buried alive in addition to the destruction of her family/state. She does not transform the state/family/ego as Deleuze and Guattari suggest the schizoid should aim for, and which Butler claims Antigone achieves. She does not become an id set free. Rather, she is frozen in a tomb in the realm of living death. That the depressive structure of state/family/ego must be resisted is not disputed. Butler is right in warning us that, as long as our culture does not accept other types of kinship, many will remain subjected to troubling violence and oppressions. The issue, however, is whether Butler, in suggesting new forms of kinship, can transform the social structure of state/family/ego and change it for the better.

What Butler forgets is that the tale of Antigone serves to remind us of the patriarchal insistence that women and nature are a real threat and that they hold the forces of total annihilation if they follow Antigone's path and we do not curb them in advance. Antigone's tragedy, I fear, continues to support deep fears and paranoia. Antigone does not resist Creon, she merely serves as the ultimate figure of what happens if one dares to resist. Her repetitious speech acts enhance our understanding that, no matter what she says, Creon does not and cannot listen; the resistances of state/family/ego are too strong. Her image cannot serve to 'free' us from an edipal structure of family/state; her sexuality is not set free but annihilated. Antigone does not find a better familial or individual lifestyle in her cave.

What is intriguing in the image of Antigone, for the modern reader who cannot find any moral support for Creon and who believes that Creon has transgressed the limits of his political jurisdiction and power, is that she or he cannot understand Antigone's action, despite her or his agreement with her moral motivation. Antigone, despite being morally on the right, remains a figure not understood. Her death does not achieve a better way of life—not for Antigone, not for her sister, and not for the citizens of her state. She remains a puzzle for the reader, an *Até* (ἄτη), as Lacan says: the limit of our understanding.[61]

---

[61] *Até*, says Lacan, "designates the limit that human life can only briefly cross" (Lacan 1992, 262). And "Antigone's position represents the radical limit that affirms the unique value of his [the human] being without any reference to any content, to whatever good or evil Polynices may have done, or to whatever he may be subjected to" (279). According to Lacan, Antigone's action cannot be understood. We can, however, see how her action causes in us a

What Antigone's action produces in the reader, despite all attempts to insist on her moral justifications, is neither a fuller understanding nor a better program for the good lifestyle. Her tale produces resistance of great force in its readers, but its does not offer a way out. It shuts the reader in; it closes in on the reader's ability to react in a positive way to the unfolding narrative. It reinforces and performs the resistances of ego, over and over again, but to the extent that ego kills its own drives. It is a paranoia-producing text for a reader who needs to be told that the norms of state/family/ego are not to be questioned. Butler promises us that the dissolution of the state and family, even sexuality, by performative deviation will set us free, just as Antigone deviates from her sexual roles as mother, wife, and daughter, but ego nonetheless retains its hold in the tragedy.

In addition, Butler does not offer us another type of ego structure that is not affected and caused by resistances. She offers no content and no mechanism by which ego can be altered. Re-enacting a variety of familial relations—heterosexual, homosexual, lesbian or queer—or performing the incest taboo in different ways does not undo the principle by which the incest taboo traps the drives—it reinforces it. By performing a variety of familial/stately gestures one does not express oneself, but rather limits oneself to a variety of the same, much like Freud's variety of Oedipal events which the Wolfman is thought to have experienced or witnessed. Performance does not resist resistances so as to find its creative force; rather, it repeats the same, it becomes a negative force which reduces any attempt to change to a single construct: Just as Antigone is buried, so are the drives shut off while they are still alive.

The family/state structures the individual, according to Deleuze and Guattari, and this doubling forms the mechanism of the 'bait' that orders the individual-to-be to shut off and make unconscious all divergent possibilities. By recasting the family/state in different forms, the social order repeats itself and enforces its reactionary forces. "Therefore, we formulate the following law," say Deleuze and Guattari:

> The father and the mother exist only as fragments, and are never organized into a figure or a structure able both to represent the unconscious, and to represent in it the various agents of the collectivity; rather, they

---

reaction, which Lacan identifies as a reaction to beauty. Antigone's beauty, he says, "dazzles us and separates us from its true function. The moving side of beauty causes all critical judgment to vacillate, stops analysis, and plunges the different forms involved into a certain confusion, or rather, an essential blindness" (281). In this case, Antigone's action, in being beautiful and that which cannot be understood, moves us and undermines the resistances we bring to the tragedy.

always shatter into fragments that come into contact with these agents, meet them face to face, square off with them, or settle the differences with them as in hand-to-hand combat. (Deleuze & Guattari 1972, 97)

What must be resisted are the reactive forces that resist the structure of family/state and yet recast it nonetheless. What must be resisted is the regime that pairs people, regardless of the types of pairs. What must be resisted is the regime that prohibits alternative forms of life. What must be resisted is a culture that directs the drives into a synthesis or an integrative whole. In other words, "Is it not more likely that Oedipus is a requirement or a consequence of social reproduction?" (13). It is a requirement of resistance.

Bibliography

Abraham, N., and M. Torok. 1986. *The Wolf Man's Magic Word.* Translated by N. Rand. Minneapolis: University of Minnesota Press, 1986.
Butler, J. 2000. *Antigone's Claim: Kinship between Life and Death.* New York: Columbia University Press, 2000.
Deleuze, G., and F. Guattari. 1972. *Anti-Oedipus: Capitalism and Schizophrenia.* Translated by R. Hurley, M. Seem and H. R. Lane. Minneapolis: University of Minnesota Press, 1983.
Derrida, J. 1998. *Resistances of Psychoanalysis.* Translated by P. Kamuf, P. A. Brault, and M. Naas. Stanford: Stanford University Press, 1998.
Freud, S. 1900. 'The Interpretation of Dreams.' SE 5.
———. 1910. 'The Future Prospects of the Psychoanalytic Therapy.' SE 11.
———. 1912. 'Recommendations to Physicians Practicing Psycho-Analysis.' SE 12.
———. 1913. 'On the Beginning the Treatment (Further Recommendations on the Technique of Psycho-Analysis.' SE 12.
———. 1914. 'Remembering, Repeating and Working-Through (Further Recommendations on the Technique of Psycho-Analysis II.' SE 12.
———. 1918. 'From the History of an Infantile Neurosis (The "Wolf Man").' SE 17.
———. 1920. 'The Psychogenesis of a Case of Female Homosexuality.' SE 18.
———. 1926. 'The Question of Lay Analysis.' SE 20.
———. 1937. 'Analysis Terminable and Interminable.' SE 23.
———. 1937. 'Constructions in Analysis.' SE 23.
Hegel, G. W. F. 1807. *The Phenomenology of Spirit.* Translated by A. V. Miller. Oxford: Oxford University Press, 1977.
Heidegger, M. 1971. "Building Dwelling Thinking." In *Poetry, Language, Thought,* 145–161. Translated by A. Hofstadter. New York: Harper and Row, 1971.

——. 1977. "The Age of the World Picture." In *The Question Concerning Technology*. Translated by William Lovitt. New York: Harper and Row, 1977, pp. 3-35.

Lacan, J. 1966. 'Agency of the Letter in the Unconscious.' In *Écrits*. Translated by A. Sheridan. New York: Norton, 1977.

——. 1978. *The Four Fundamental Concepts of Psycho-Analysis*. Translated by A. Sheridan. New York: Norton, 1978.

——. 1988. *Freud's Papers on Techniques*. Translated by J. Forrester. Cambridge: Cambridge University Press, 1988.

——. 1992. *The Ethics of Psychoanalysis, 1959–1960*. Translated by D. Porter. New York: Norton, 1992.

Muller, J. P., and W. J. Richardson, eds. 1988. *The Purloined Poe*. Baltimore: Johns Hopkins University Press, 1988.

Nancy, J.-L., and P. Lacoue-Labarthe. 1992. *The Title of the Letter*. Translated by F. Raiffoul and D. Pettigrew. New York: State University of New York Press, 1992.

Literature as Symptomatology: Gilles Deleuze on Sacher-Masoch

Tomas Geyskens

For authors, if they are great, are more like doctors than patients.
(Deleuze 1969, 273)

Gilles Deleuze's *Coldness and Cruelty* (1967) is a fascinating analysis of the literary works of Leopold von Sacher-Masoch but has no relevance for the *clinical* understanding of masochism. With this appeal to a clear-cut distinction between literature and clinical practice, psychoanalysts have all too easily dismissed Deleuze's critique of Freud's theory of masochism (Laplanche 1980, 297). Freudians who invoke the distinction between the literary and the clinical as if this distinction goes without saying, should raise our suspicion. After all, it was Sigmund Freud who liberated the study of the neuroses from the straitjacket of scientific positivism by trying to understand hysteria from the perspective of literature. Already in his *Studies on Hysteria* (1895) Freud is very clear about the intimate and inevitable link between literature and clinical psychoanalysis:

> I have not always been a psychotherapist. Like other neuro-pathologists, I was trained to employ local diagnoses and electro-prognosis, and it still strikes me myself as strange that the case histories I write should read like *short stories* and that, as one might say, *they lack the serious stamp of science*. I must console myself with the reflection that *the nature of the subject* is evidently responsible for this, rather than any preference of my own. The fact is that local diagnosis and electrical reactions lead nowhere in the study of hysteria, whereas a detailed description of mental processes such as we are accustomed to find *in the works of imaginative writers* enables me, with the use of a few psychological formulas, to obtain at least some kind of insight into the course of that affection. (SE 2, 160–161; my italics)

The origin of psychoanalysis as a clinical practice is unthinkable without this transition from serious science to short story, a transition which does not depend on a bent for the poetic on Freud's part but on 'the nature of the subject' [*die Natur des Gegenstandes*] (cf. de Certeau 1987, 121). Analysing

Sacher-Masoch's novels as a way to criticise Freud's theory of masochism does not constitute a break with psychoanalytic methodology; on the contrary, it renews a gesture that belongs to the original core of Freud's clinical thinking.

To understand the clinical relevance of Deleuze's reading of Masoch we must ask another question: with *what kind of* literature and with *what kind of* clinic do Freud and Deleuze deal? Freud thinks of a specific kind of clinic, that of the neuroses, from the perspective of a specific kind of literature, Sophocles' *Oedipus Rex* and Shakespeare's *Hamlet*. In *The Logic of Sense* (1969) Deleuze writes:

> An evaluation of symptoms might be achieved only through a *novel*. It is not by chance that the neurotic creates a 'familial romance,' and that the Oedipus complex must be found in the meanderings of it. From the perspective of Freud's genius, it is not the complex which provides us with information about Oedipus and Hamlet, but rather Oedipus and Hamlet who provide us with information about the complex. (Deleuze 1969, 237; italics in the original)

Freud's literary clinic is a clinic of neurosis, and it is at this point that Deleuze's critique of Freud must be situated: Freud does not think about sadism and masochism from the perspective of the literature of perversion, but he construes these perversions from the perspective of neurosis, from the idea that neurosis is the negative of perversion. It is this construction-from-neurosis which leads Freud to the idea that sadism and masochism are two poles of *one* perversion: sado-masochism. Deleuze's critical-clinical reading of Sade and Masoch is one long attack on this Freudian notion.

Sadomasochism does not belong to the world of perversion, but in the symptomatology of neurosis. When Jean Laplanche defends Freud against Deleuze, he argues that sadomasochism is an undeniable fact ... in the clinic of obsessional neurosis: "These underlying structures are also present in neurosis, and *maybe even more clearly in neurosis* than in perversion (which is another point that Deleuze does not even mention)" (Laplanche 1980, 294; italics in the original). Laplanche's criticism of Deleuze actually proves the latter's point: psychoanalysis understands perversion from the perspective of neurosis and in this way 'neuroticizes' the perversions. It is this 'neurotic' perspective that leads Freud to the non-entity 'sadomasochism.' The fact that the unpleasure of the neurotic's self-torture must actually be understood as a pleasure that cannot be experienced as such, as an unconscious 'sadomasochism,' does not teach us anything about sadism and masochism as perversions.

Freud repeatedly stated that the poets have always had an intuitive feeling for the unconscious, but this never motivated him to read Sade or

Masoch. There is no indication to be found that he ever read their works. Such a reading would have changed his ideas about sadism and masochism in a radical way. This is at least the underlying assumption of Deleuze's interpretation of Masoch's works. For Deleuze, Sade and Masoch are not just perverts; they are also the great clinicians of perversion. They were the first ones to describe a new and aberrant sexuality and, in so doing, they developed new ways of feeling, writing, and thinking (Deleuze 1967, 16). The worlds these literary clinicians construe, are worlds-without-Other. Sade and Masoch open a radical alternative for a way of living which is a priori structured by and subjected to the Other. For Deleuze, perversion is first of all a 'strange Spinozism' (Deleuze 1969, 359).

To understand Deleuze's thoughts on perversion, we must first unmask the illusion of sadomasochism, the illusion that sadism and masochism are two complementary tendencies that mirror each other.

* * *

Sadism and masochism are two totally different, non-complementary worlds. Even a superficial reading of Sade's *120 Days of Sodom* (1784) and Masoch's *Venus in Furs* (1870) shows immediately that there can be no question of complementarity or of a possible encounter. Already on the level of pornographic descriptions there is a fundamental difference between Sade's monotonous repetitions of the most extreme obscenities described in detailed, mechanical and anatomical terms and the prudish and suggestive language of Masoch who only evokes a suffocating erotic atmosphere without ever revealing anything or naming anything by name. This difference on the level of description points towards a more fundamental difference. Let us first read Sade.

In Sade's novels, the pornographic descriptions are not aimed at erotic excitation. If this were the case, these novels would only appeal to the sexual taste of a 'happy' few. This would not disturb us very much. But Sade's obscene descriptions are directed by a porno-logical programme, not by pornographic enthusiasm. It is Sade's aim to correspond to and to participate in the cold, destructive force of Nature through a rationalistic-spinozist demonstration. Nature, which lets itself be known to us in enjoyment, does not halt at the conventional limits of disgust, shame, and morality. Even the incest taboo and the prohibition of murder are only conventional obstacles that keep us from obeying the voice of reason, which is the voice of our true nature (Deleuze 1967, 18).

Sade is an exponent of eighteenth-century materialism and rationalism. This philosophy demands that we free ourselves from all illusions and idols, and that we start living according to truth, even if this truth seems to contradict our subjective perceptions and our affective experiences. Sade's demonstrations show how much such a philosophy is soaked in an ascetic ideal and thus in cruelty. Sadism is the rationalist ascetics of becoming insensitive towards conventions, taboos, and superstitions. Sade's programme is not aimed at some personal, sexual preference, but at an impersonal apathy: the enjoyment promised by sadism is an impersonal, ascetic enjoyment in rational demonstration, which makes us insensitive towards our personal tastes and interests. The impersonal enjoyment of pure reason destroys the personal affectivity of the ego—hence Sade's contempt for those who are sexually excited by torture. The sadist's aim is not to be sexually excited by torturing other people, but to put one's cold-bloodedness and insensitivity to the test of torture without regressing to cruelty or pity. Sade is porno *more geometrico*. Even when the sadist tortures himself, this is not an indication of some intimate intertwining of sadism and masochism; it only means that the sadist's own pain has become the ultimate test of his apathy, which participates in the cold indifference of pure Reason (Deleuze 1967, 29).

The ascetic ideal of Sade's rationalism produces a cruel and all-powerful Super-Ego. To elucidate the role played by the Super-Ego in sadism, Deleuze starts from Freud's view, in which the Super-Ego is the heir of the father and the manifestation of the drive for self-destruction. In sadism, the destructive power of the Super-Ego has acquired such force that it completely takes over the Ego. The Super-Ego becomes Almighty and the Ego is projected in the external world, in the victims of the sadist. The sadist has no Ego anymore, except in his victims. Only in the victims (cf. Justine) do the personal and the affective survive (Deleuze 1967, 124).

This splitting between Ego and Super-Ego, and the projection of the Ego that accompanies this splitting, have a remarkable effect on the meaning of the Super-Ego. For Freud, the Super-Ego represents morality and the Oedipal father who prohibits the incestuous relation with the mother. For Deleuze, however, the moral character of the Super-Ego is an illusion produced by the fact that the conflict between the Ego and the Super-Ego remains *intra-psychic*, as is always the case in Freud. But, when the Ego is projected in the external world and the Super-Ego can unleash all its violence on the external victims who now contain the sadist's Ego, the Super-Ego shows its true nature. It loses all its moral connotations and shows itself as the obscene and sadistic force it always already was (Deleuze 1967, 124).

How should we understand this ironic unmasking of the Super-Ego concretely? What kind of father is this sadistic Super-Ego the heir of? For Freud, the Super-Ego is the heir of the father of the Oedipus complex, who excludes the child from the sexual relation between father and mother. In this way, the father becomes the keeper of the incest taboo and of the morality of which this taboo is the kernel. In sadism, this Oedipal structure is turned upside down. The Oedipal prohibition is grounded in the sexual interest of the father for the mother. But the daughter knows better. Actually, the father is only *pater familias* by social conformism. This conformism only hides the incestuous father who prefers his daughter over his wife, and who incites his daughter to liquidate her mother. Against the moralistic *pater familias* is the sadistic-apathic *pater sive Natura*. The father, in an incestuous relationship with his daughter, aims at the destruction of the mother, the family, and the law; he represents the true, anarchic, destructive force of Nature. From Sade's point of view, the Freudian Oedipus complex is merely a neurotic phantasm, an expression of the social conformism and the sexual discontent of the neurotic. Sadism shows that the father does not belong on the side of the family, morality, and reproductive sexuality, but in a sodomite alliance with the daughter against the mother. This destruction of the existing order should not be interpreted too piously as an enjoyment in transgression. The apathic enjoyment Sade evokes is a direct expression of the indifferent destructiveness of Nature. The enjoyment of the sadist is not in the transgression of the moral order, but in the *participation* in apathic nature. The self-preservation of the Ego, the reproduction in the family, and the laws of morality are not capable of expressing this Nature adequately. Their destruction is only the effect, not the aim, of sadistic enjoyment (Deleuze 1967, 59–60).

* * *

Sadism is a very specific rationalistic-naturalistic programme that has nothing in common with the world of masochism. We already mentioned the differences in style, sphere, and terminology between Sade and Masoch. Sade's monotonous catalogue of obscenities has nothing in common with Masoch's art of suggestion, postponement, and suspense. Masoch's décor is one of frozen images, stills, theatrical gestures that are suspended in the moment *before* something will happen. It is a world without movement, the 'dynamics' of which are described by Freud in his article on *Fetishism* (1927).

When the little boy in the phallic phase is confronted with sexual difference, or rather, with the absence of the female penis, he interprets this absence as a lack. The sight of the female genitals convinces him that the threat of castration is a real danger. This traumatic event then becomes the motive of repression and (infantile) neurosis. But this scenario is avoided by the fetishist-to-be, who is able to *disavow* the perception of the female genitals. This disavowal must be understood as a cinematographic procedure rather than as a psychological mechanism. Disavowal is not some sort of denial or subtle self-deception. Freud describes disavowal as the suspension of sexual curiosity at 'the last impression before the uncanny and traumatic one' (SE 21, 155). That is why fur and velvet are ideal materials to become fixated as fetishes: "Fur and velvet—as has long been suspected—are a fixation of the sight of the pubic hair, which should have been followed by the longed-for sight of the female member; pieces of underclothing, which are so often chosen as a fetish, *crystallise the moment of undressing, the last moment* in which the woman could still be regarded as phallic" (155; my italics). The genital is not denied or repressed, but suspended and deferred forever.

According to Deleuze, Freud's mini-myth of the fetishist boy contains, at least implicitly, all the elements that constitute the world of masochism. This is not surprising. Fetishism is an essential part of masochism. Masoch's masterpiece is not by accident *Venus in Furs*. The disavowal of the female genitals produces, first of all, an idealisation of the woman as a cold mother goddess without desire, who wants nothing. When Freud describes this ideal of female self-sufficiency in *On Narcissism* (1914), he refers, very much in the style of Masoch, to "the charm of certain animals which seem not to concern themselves about us, such as cats and the large beasts of prey" (SE 14, 89). It is this ideal, sexually self-sufficient woman who is staged by Masoch in frozen poses and photographic gestures, in the endlessly suspended moment *before* the fur will fall and reveal the female body, in the moment *before* the whip will strike the gagged slave. The fetishist disavowal takes the woman out of the movement of genital sexuality and isolates her in an imaginary world of frozen stills. This *freezing* of the woman then turns back on the sexuality of the man. The spontaneous directness towards genital satisfaction is not so much suppressed but deferred and frozen in an endless suspense (Deleuze 1967, 33–34).

The disavowal of the female genitals has a catastrophic effect on the function of the father. The discovery of the castration of the mother is a crucial moment in the normal sexual development of the boy because this discovery shows that the threat of castration, which is attributed to the father, better be taken seriously. But the disavowal of the castration of the mother neutralises the Oedipal father and his threat. The father is 'foreclosed' from the masochist's world. Deleuze goes radically against Freud's idea that the father, although absent from the manifest content of male masochism, is hidden behind the mother or the mistress in the unconscious fantasy (SE 17, 198). For Deleuze, this Freudian construction is the consequence of his false idea that masochism is the reverse of sadism. In the sadistic fantasy the incestuous father plays the leading role, and that is why Freud must believe that the father is also the central figure in masochism. But in masochism the father is foreclosed and his power is transferred to the mother.

My mother beats me, but not to satisfy my feeling of guilt or my need for punishment. The mistress humiliates and beats me because I still resemble my father, because I am still the bearer of this ridiculous sign of genital sexuality, the phallus. The mother does not so much beat the son; she beats the father in the son; she beats the father out of the son. Masochism is a Spartan education and the aim of this educational process is the production of a new man 'without father and without sexuality.' The horizon of masochism is the rebirth of an a-phallic creature out of the mother alone (Deleuze, 1967, 64–66).

Of course, this disavowal of genital sexuality in fetishism and masochism cannot reach a state of actual a-sexuality. Fetishism and masochism belong from beginning to end to the sphere of sexuality. Masochism aims at an *other sexuality* than the genital one that is directed towards satisfaction and always refers to reproduction and to the role of the father. To describe this 'other sexuality' in a positive way, we must first focus on some other aspects of masochism.

* * *

To construct his masochistic world, in which nothing can be left to spontaneity or chance, the masochist relies on a *contract*. Every aspect of the masochistic ritual is stipulated in the contract and nothing should happen that is not prescribed beforehand. The masochistic contract has a double function. On the one hand, it educates the woman in how to become an Ideal. The contract allows the masochist to model the mistress into the ideal woman of his imagination: she has to wear fur, she must express her severity and cruelty in very specific ways which are stipulated by the contract, she should not enjoy the humiliation and the torture sadistically, et cetera. The masochistic contract situates the ideal woman between two positions: she should not succumb to the easy pleasures of genital satisfaction but neither should she regress to the sadistic position of the one who *enjoys* torturing. Masoch's ideal is located between these two positions, in what Deleuze describes as 'the cold, oral mother.' In masochism, the mother is cold, severe, and sentimental like Mother Earth who feeds and kills, and to whom, in the end, all her children return. She is a cold and severe mother, but not a sadistic woman (Deleuze, 1967, 55).

The second function of the contract is the perpetuation of the foreclosure of the father. In masochism, the father is not repressed but foreclosed. This implies that the father does not return in a symbolic, distorted way *in* the masochistic fantasy, but that his hallucinatory return is the end *of* the fantasy. This 'psychotic' destruction of the masochistic fantasy is described in the final scene of *Venus in Furs*. Wanda introduces a man who enjoys beating Severin, and now Wanda becomes the sadistic ally of this man. But this turn of the story was not stipulated by the contract. In the sadist who tortures Severin, the father, who was foreclosed from the masochist's world, returns. This hallucinatory return of the father does not reveal the hidden meaning of masochism. On the contrary, it is the destruction of the fantasy and the implosion of the masochistic universe. After this scene, Severin is 'cured' (Deleuze 1967, 65).

That the father is not repressed but foreclosed also implies that the masochist does not suffer from a feeling of guilt, not even an 'unconscious' one. The father is thrown out of the masochistic world and his power is transferred by the masochist to the mother. Thereby, the Super-Ego has lost its power. The references to a crime that must be punished belong to the humour of masochism; the only 'crime' of the masochist is that he still resembles his father; that is the crime of the masochist, the crime of the father in the son.

* * *

Masoch's masochism does not only dominate his sexual life; it is his whole way of feeling, writing, and thinking. This power of masochism to dominate the entire life and mind of the individual should not be understood in a Freudian way as a symptom or a sublimation. A tendency to get hold of even the smallest aspect of psychic life and to put its stamp on it, is essential to the drive as such. This expansion of the drive's power is accompanied by a process of depersonalisation. To elucidate this idea, we must refer to a small text by Sacher-Masoch, 'A Childhood Memory and Reflections on the Novel,' from 1888.

Masoch distinguishes three moments in the constitution of his masochistic desire. First there is a particular, innate disposition, which always already isolated the subject from the others. As a child already, Leopold is fascinated by the cruel histories about saints and martyrs. These stories make a dark impression and awaken a feverish nervousness in him, the first sign of a deep desire. This particular disposition then waits for a good occasion that will set it on fire and crystallise it into an *idée fixe* (Deleuze 1967, 275).

When he was ten years old, he adored the beautiful and gallant countess Zénobie, a distant relative of his father. On a certain day, when the countess caught him while he was spying on her, she gave him a thrashing with a whip. She wore a fur coat while doing this. Leopold had tears in his eyes, but at the same time he experienced 'acute pleasure': "This event became engraved on my soul as with a red-hot iron" (Deleuze 1967, 275). Leopold's encounter with countess Zénobie is certainly not a traumatic accident; it is rather an event that resonates with Masoch's instinctual disposition. The event gives the drives a prototype and a particular constellation, so that it can become an obsession which absorbs Masoch's desire completely. Every new event and encounter will now appear in the strange, dark light of this obsessive fantasy.

In the third moment which Masoch distinguishes, he breaks radically with the psychoanalytic treatment of the fantasy. A psychoanalytic perspective would try to diminish the obsessive power of the fantasy by relating it again to the personal history of the subject or to confront it with symbolic castration as the supra-personal truth of desire. Masoch proposes another procedure: transforming the fantasy into an ideological structure.

Masoch reads Bachofen. In *Das Mutterrecht*, Bachofen paints a grandiose vision of human history. Before patriarchy, there was a period of matriarchy. Within this matriarchal period, there was a first phase characterised by the promiscuous sexuality of the swamps, where the father was unknown and unimportant, and then a second period of reclamation of the swamps, agriculture, and matriarchal power in the steppe. The father has a certain status but remains subordinate to the mother. Bachofen relates the first period to Aphrodite, and the second to Demeter. These matriarchal periods were then succeeded by the patriarchal order of the modern age, the period of Apollo. In the ancient myths and legends, Bachofen finds traces of the conflict between matriarchy and patriarchy everywhere. For instance, he considers the cult of Dionysos a return of the repressed mother-religions in the period of patriarchy.

In the figure of Demeter, the goddess of the second matriarchal period, Masoch discovers his ideal of a cold, severe Mother, whose coldness resists the cheerful paganism of Aphrodite and whose motherliness goes against the patriarchal order of Apollo. In Masoch's reading of Bachofen, the mother goddess Demeter enters into a strange alliance with Aunt Zénobie: "Here the fantasy finds what it needs, namely a theoretical and ideological structure which transforms it into a general conception of human nature and of the world" (Deleuze 1967, 53). The personal fantasy is projected onto the impersonal myth. In this way, an identity is established between the mother, the steppe, and nature, characterised by severity, coldness, and motherliness. But this masochistic projection of Zénobie onto Nature must be distinguished from the Freudian conception of projection.

In 'The Economic Problem of Masochism' (1924) Freud shows that, in the course of development, the parental imagos are transferred onto other authority figures such as teachers and heroes, and even onto impersonal forces such as Destiny, Nature, and Death. Even these impersonal forces receive the features of the parents of our childhood. Few are able to resist such a *personification* of the impersonal, says Freud (SE 19, 168). At first sight, Masoch's transference of Zénobie onto Nature is such a personification of nature. Nature becomes like a mother figure from Masoch's childhood. But, the Freudian interpretation misses the *double* movement of this projection. What happens is not only a personification of Nature, but also a depersonalisation of the people in one's own history. The figure of Aunt Zénobie is projected onto Nature as Steppe and Ice-Age. Nature receives the features of a mother, of Mother Earth who—severe and cold, but without hatred—feeds and kills her own children. This is the Freudian projection. But what Freud neglects is the reverse movement: the identity Mother – Steppe – Nature also depersonalises Zénobie, who now receives the impersonal features of the cold, severe motherliness of the Earth. This movement of depersonalisation causes a shift from a metaphoric to a metonymic level. Zénobie is not only *like* Nature, she is also part *of* Nature. She represents the Steppe, but she also *participates* in the Steppe.

This projection/participation transforms the relationship of the subject to his fantasy. My personal obsessions and symptoms lose their connection with my individual history and become impersonal. My symptoms now repeat timeless traits of Nature. Masoch's personal obsession becomes the expression of the eternal affinity between passion and cruelty (Deleuze 1967, 276). The projection of the fantasy onto the myth is not a defence or rationalisation. It does not diminish the power of the obsessive fantasy, but feeds the obsession and makes it stronger. The alliance with Bachofen enables Masoch to express his sexuality in *all* aspects of life. The symptom becomes a way of life and manifests itself in Masoch's political, religious, and artistic ideas. Masoch's symptom becomes a literary style of suggestion and suspense, a political ideal of a pan-Slavic matriarchal communism, and a remarkable Christology. Not the Son, but the Father, dies at the Cross. The Son is taken from the Cross by the Virgin Mother, who stages the whole Passion. The Pieta as the truth of the Crucifixion: "It is the Mother who crucifies the Son; in the masochistic elaboration of the Marean fantasy, the Virgin in person puts Christ on the cross. It is not the son who dies so much as God the Father, that is the likeness of the father in the son" (Deleuze 1967, 97).

The transformation of the personal fantasy into a Naturalism of the Oral Mother is a process of depersonalisation. The Ego is not replaced by an apathic Super-Ego, as in sadism, but it dissolves into a mythic world where sexuality has surrendered to the cold charms of the Steppe.

* * *

Deleuze describes Masoch's de-genitalisation of sexuality as a 'de-sexualisation.' He follows Masoch's words about 'a new man without father and without sexuality.' This formulation, however, wrongly suggests that masochism would be a kind of spirituality. Masochism is not a sublimation or a desexualisation, but an internal transformation of sexuality. Sexuality is degenitalised in favour of another sexuality.

In *The Logic of Sense*, Deleuze presents *Vendredi ou les limbes du Pacifique*, a novel by Michel Tournier. In this novel Tournier re-writes the story of Robinson Crusoe to show the real effects of a world without Other. After the shipwreck, Robinson lives alone on a small island. What interests Tournier is not so much the fact that there are no other people on the island, but that Robinson becomes more and more detached from the Other-as-structure who structures the human world a priori. This detachment from the Other has very severe effects on Robinson's perception, desire, and sexuality. It produces a radical depersonalisation in Robinson. According to Deleuze, Tournier's literary experiment has close affinities with the problem of perversion. The pervert, too, lives on a small island in a world-without-Other:

> Is not this progressive though irreversible dissolution of the structure what the pervert, on his interior 'isle', attains by other means? To put it in Lacanian terms, the 'forclusion' of Others brings it about that others are no longer apprehended as Others, since the structure which would give them this place and this function is missing. But is it not then the whole of our perceived world that collapses in the interest of something else ... ? (Deleuze 1969, 349)

Deleuze's suggestion that the pervert lives in a dehumanised world which is no longer structured by the Other allows us to understand the different components of masochism, and the element in which they must be situated. The dissolution of the Other transforms the pervert's relation to the objects, to the other, and to himself.

The objectivity of objects is constituted by the perspective of the Other. The possibility of another perspective introduces a lack in the real: what I see becomes a sign of what I do not see but can see when I join the perspective of the Other. This introduction of another perspective gives things their depth. Now things cover each other, are covered by each other, and relate to each other as to a horizon. Each object appears against the background of other objects, and can, in its turn, become the background for another object. Each object can therefore always be dis-covered and explored further because the Other opens possible perspectives which are already actual as possibilities in my perception. The Other-as-structure is the unactualised reality of possible worlds (Deleuze 1969, 344–345).

Fetishism is misunderstood when the fetish is considered as an *object*, an object in which the fetishist then sees mysterious qualities invisible to others. In this 'objective' view, fetishism is introduced in an element that is radically alien to the world of perversion: the adoration of objects that are associatively linked with the loved one. The lover is only interested in the glove or the hair clippings of his loved one because these objects evoke the unexplored world of the beloved. The loved one is a possible world and love and jealousy are attempts to explore this world (Deleuze 1969, 347). In his analysis of fetishism Freud had already remarked that perverse fetishism should be distinguished from this 'fetishism of love' because in perverse fetishism the fetish becomes isolated from its context of reference (SE 7, 154). With Deleuze's analysis, this 'isolation' of the fetish can be described more clearly. The pervert lives in a world-without-Other, and in such a 'world' objects start to lose their referring function. They are not the announcement of a world anymore:

The fetish is therefore not a symbol at all, but as it were a frozen, arrested, two-dimensional image, a photograph to which one returns repeatedly to exorcise the dangerous consequences of movement, the harmful discoveries that result from exploration. (Deleuze 1967, 31)

> The fetish of the pervert and the glove of the loved one have totally different functions: the glove *opens* a world of possibilities; the fetish *stops* the movement of exploration and reduces objects to a pure surface, a photographic world without depth or possibility. In the world of the pervert, there is nothing to explore or to discover, least of all the traces of the loved one. To the poetic depth of love, the pervert opposes a photographic erotics of surfaces.

The objects lose their signifying function because the Other is destroyed. The mistress in masochism is not another subject. Masochism is not an intersubjective relation. In perversion, the other does not function as an Other who structures the world as a world of possible perspectives. Perversion is a radical de-subjectivation of the other. This de-subjectivation is misunderstood in psychological theories of perversion. According to these theories, perversion is characterised by hatred for the Other; hatred which is expressed in actions which objectify and dehumanise the Other. These theories miss the point because they locate the destruction of the Other on the level of psychological motives and criminal acts. But the 'murder of the Other' does not belong primarily to the content of perversion; it is, rather, presupposed in the world of the pervert (Deleuze 1969, 359). Masoch's mistress is not another subject who makes the world into a world of perspectives that can be explored. The mistress in masochism is only an 'element' in the pervert's strange Spinozism:

> The world of the pervert is a world without Others, and thus a world without the possible. The Other is that which renders possible. The perverse world is a world in which the category of the necessary has completely replaced that of the possible. This is a strange Spinozism

from which 'oxygen' is lacking, to the benefit of a more elementary energy and a more rarified air. (Deleuze 1969, 359)

This world without Other and without possibility is not merely a pathological aberration; it is an adventure and a way out (Deleuze 1969, 348). The one who falls from the world of the Other finds another 'world,' a desubjectivised sphere of forces and elements, a photographic erotics of pure intensities: "The pure surface is perhaps what Others were hiding from us" (Deleuze 1969, 354).

In *A Thousand Plateaus*, Deleuze and Guattari present a masochist who lets himself be trained like a horse by his mistress. This mistress has to wear riding boots because the legs of a woman inevitably evoke the dynamics of genital sexuality and the possibility of exploration. But the boots belong to the atmosphere of masochism: "Legs are still organs, but the boots now only determine a zone of intensity as an imprint or zone on a body without organs" (Deleuze & Guattari 1980, 156).

Bibliography

Certeau, M. de. 1987. *Histoire et psychanalyse entre science et fiction*. Paris: Folio, 1987.
Deleuze, G. 1967. *Coldness and Cruelty*. Translated by J. McNeil. New York: Zone Books, 1989.
———. 1969. *The Logic of Sense*. Translated by M. Lester. London: Continuum, 2001.
Deleuze, G., and F. Guattari. 1980. *Capitalism and Schizophrenia: A Thousand Plateaus*. Translated by B. Massumi. Minneapolis: University of Minnesota Press, 1987.
Freud, S. 1895. 'Studies on Hysteria.' SE 2.
———. 1905. 'Three Essays on the Theory of Sexuality.' SE 7.
———. 1914. 'On Narcissism: An Introduction.' SE 14.
———. 1919. 'A Child is Being Beaten.' SE 17.
———. 1927. 'Fetishism.' SE 21.
Laplanche, J. 1980. *Problématiques 1. L'angoisse*. Paris: PUF, 1980.

Deleuze with Masoch

Éric Alliez

1. *Whether it is a question, indeed, of being oneself, being a father, being born, being loved, or being death, how can we fail to see that the subject, assuming he is the subject who speaks, sustains himself there only on the basis of discourse? It is thus clear that analysis reveals that the phallus serves the function of signifying the lack of being [*manque à être*] that is wrought in the subject by his relation to the signifier.*
(Lacan 1966, 594–595)

2. *Chatting with him, I had sought to 'discover' and discern in his words the truth of 'literature,' but now everything is blurry and I can no longer recover it.*
(Wanda von Sacher Masoch 1906)

3. *Obviously, once again, it is more than a matter of vocabulary ...*
(Deleuze 1977a, 130)

-1. *Take the case of* S.A.D.E. *[...] On the background of a static recitation of Sade's texts, it is the sadistic image of the Master which finds itself amputated, paralysed, reduced to a masturbatory tic, at the same time as the masochist Servant finds himself, develops himself, metamorphoses himself, experiments himself, constitutes himself on the stage in function of the insufficiencies of the master. The Servant is not at all the inverted image of the master, and neither is he his repetition or his contradictory identity: he is constituted piece by piece, bit by bit, from the neutralisation of the master; he acquires his autonomy from the amputation of the master.*
(Deleuze & Bene 1979, 89–90)

A question thrown to the children of the expired century: literature, what is it for, how does it work, and so on?

There is an answer that engages Deleuze *into* literature, in the guise of an inevitable *from where it leads* [*d'où ça mène*]: literature, when it works, serves to *annul the father and his lack (of being)* [*manque (à-être)*] *and his death (Death)* [*la Mort*] *(this non-being from which every negation is fuelled by a symbolisation).*

On the basis of this line to be drawn over the father [*de ce trait à tirer sur le père*], of this practical necessity of annulment, independent of any aesthetic

Éric Alliez

intention, we can state the following corollary: implicating signs in becomings that are as singular as they are impersonal, literature only moves forward by *derailing*, by *disorganising* itself, through the forces thus freed from the agency [*instance*] of the letter, from the neurotic principle of literary autonomy and the passion of the signifier that is manifested in it through linguistics.

As an absolute un-binding of the powers [*puissances*] of life from the power [*pouvoir*] of the father, and through a radical dis-identification from the names of the Father, the critique of psychoanalysis will—by a kind of Deleuzean consequence—be indissociable from a *literary clinic*, replacing the scene of writing with the subtraction, the *minoration* of literature 'itself' (*La littérature?*). This will even be its 'test,' the evaluation immanent to the exercise of non-style of *a* literature: *that words, to make a sensation, owe it to us and to themselves no longer to make 'Text,'* in this course that would have led them from symbolism to the Symbolic by way of another trinity ... *Wankers (branleurs) of the Name-of-the-father*—this provocative assertion, which might have once stirred Lacan, disqualifies the '*matérialistes*' of the labour of the signifier and other assorted logothetes of the textual act.

Knowing that the French scene was haunted by the inflation of the 'Sadean text,' whose pornographic autonomy—'a textual book, textured of pure writing' (Barthes 1971, 35)[62]—rushes into a *sado-modernism*, Deleuze acquires the autonomy of his difference with regard to the new masters (*we are in 1967*[63]) in 'One Manifesto Less' (*avant la lettre*),[64] whose first title, mixing grace and disgrace, is as follows: *Presentation of Sacher Masoch: Coldness and Cruelty*. (But Deleuze had already published in 1961 a *very first* article entitled 'From Sacher-Masoch to Masochism.') Through this 'literary approach' (Deleuze 1967, 14) from which it came to be named ('masochism'), through its retroactive effect engaging in new relations, 'the critical (in the literary sense) and the clinical (in the medical sense),' through this name taken against the grain of its common, victimological meaning (*Coldness and Cruelty*), in order to give its due to a 'refinement of symptomatology' (Deleuze 1967, 16) other than the one provided by Sadean anthropology, some were shocked to see "that even the most enlightened psychoanalytic writers link the emergence of

---

[62] R. Barthes, ' L'arbre du crime,' *Tel Quel* 28 (Winter 1967); and volume XVI of Sade's *Œuvres complètes*, reprinted in Barthes 1971 ('Sade I'). It is in this same re-edition of the *Œuvres complètes* of Sade, in the postface to volume III, that is reprinted Lacan's article 'Kant avec Sade' (*Critique* 191 [April 1963]): "In which it is demonstrated [...] that desire is the obverse of the law."

[63] See *Tel Quel* 28 (Winter 1967), 'La pensée de Sade' (Klossowski/Barthes/Sollers/Damisch/Tort).

[64] 'One Manifesto Less' is the title given by Deleuze to his text from *Superpositions*, with Carmelo Bene, whose key passage, from pp. 89–90, we have used as one of our epigraphs (Deleuze & Bene 1979).

a symbolic order with the 'name of the father'" (Deleuze 1967a, 63). Because the mother, far from being of nature, is "the condition for the symbolism through which the masochist expresses himself"; because a woman-lacking-nothing [*femme-ne-manquant-de-rien*] goddess is at the heart of the 'art of the fantasy' that characterises these *trompe l'oeil* constructions that command the very thing that the phallocentric law was intended to prohibit ... For the misunderstanders [*les mal-entendants*] of the blows aimed at the father—since "*it is not a child, but a father that is being beaten*" (Deleuze 1967, 66), and it is a masochist who, blow by blow, is rendered "free for a new birth in which the father plays no role" *and the signifier does not either*[65] (Lacan 1958a, 345)— in 1989, on the pages of the newspaper *Libération*, the Presentation will be followed by a 'Re-presentation of Masoch.' Masoch's 'contributions to the art of the novel,' Deleuze reiterates, pertain to a 'diagnostic of the world' that can only lead to 'the eventual birth of a new man' through a *politics of language* (*langue*) carried to its limit in a 'body-language' whose map is not psychosomatic but 'world-historical.' It is a question of telling us that *it* [*ça*] implicates the *Anti-Oedipus* (at the price, it is true, of a radical desymbolisation and of a singular machination of Jungian animation), no less than Kafka, with these protocols of experience carried out by the one who is *not* the speaking-subject-of-his-language (Masoch, mixed in lineage and place of birth, as well as foreign to the German language, "poisons German literature" with his *Galician Tales*). Now, the Kafka-effect (*Towards a Minor Literature*)—an effect that cannot be conceived of apart from Kafka's own homage to Masoch—is the component of passage toward the *Thousand Plateaus* of the Deleuze and Guattari multiplicity, such as it took the risk of amputating the father's name, *all the names whereby the only event left would be the event of saying* (the Father as naming, the Name as ex-istence: Lacan with Heidegger), in order to give writing over to the outside: "In sum, we think that writing will never be done enough in the name of an outside" (Deleuze & Guattari 1980, 23).[66]

* * *

---

[65] Let us recall that Lacan interprets the Freudian text on the fantasy 'A child is being beaten ...' as making present the seizure of the subject on the part of the phallus-signifier. (See Lacan 1958a, 345).

[66] Bio-bibliographical Note. - 'Re-presentation of Masoch' (*Libération* [May 1989]) makes up Ch. 7 of *Essays Critical and Clinical* (pp. 53–55). (See p. 55n.3 for the analysis of the name of Gregor Samsa, the hero of the *Metamorphosis*, as a homage to Masoch.) 'Coldness and Cruelty,' published with the unabridged text of *Venus in Furs* in 1967, begins with this phrase: 'What are the uses of literature?' (p. 15): 'A quoi sert la littérature?'. The following is of essential significance for our approach: the first presentation of the masochist motif was published as early as 1961 under the title 'De Sacher-Masoch au masochisme' (*Arguments* 21), and thus coincided with the publication of the dissertation of J. Laplanche, *Hölderlin et la question du*

Éric Alliez

An outside whose character is less experimentally French—Blanchot deploying language as 'the shared transparency of the origin and death'[67] *(Foucault 1966, 58)—than oriental, but taken back from the East through the West on the American 'map.' An outside that surges up when it is a question of highlighting that everything is played out 'in the middle' [au milieu], and that, all in all, a rhizome-writing is made up of 'plateaus,' in the sense proposed by Gregory Bateson, which is summed up in the following lines: "a continuous, self-vibrating region of intensities whose development avoids any orientation toward a culmination point or external end" (Deleuze & Guattari 1980, 22). The example retained by Deleuze and Guattari is that of the mother-infant sexual games practiced in Balinese culture, in which—this is the sole quotation from Bateson—"Some sort of continuing plateau of intensity is substituted for [sexual] climax" (22).*[68] *Thousand Plateaus is of a superior masochism, a kind of Tao-masochism freed from the fantasies of the Self [Moi] and rendered to its continuums of intensities by a Body without Orgasm.*

---

père (Laplanche 1961). This was the first monograph by a student of Lacan to apply the theory of the Name-of-the-Father by confronting it with the schizophrenia that the poet opens up as a question, when he touched on the 'paradox of *warming oneself with ice*,' of 'finding his comfort in the *absolute cold*, his support in absolute distance' (pp. 58–59)—whence 'an equilibrating function of Hölderlinian poetry and myth,' which no longer designates, in the absence of the father, the source of all evils (p. 132). In the Deleuzean chronology, 1961 means prior to the first edition of *Proust and Signs* (from 1964), a work entirely traversed by a critique of philosophy to the extent that the latter 'is ignorant to the dark regions in which are elaborated the effective forces that act on thought, the determinations that *force* us to think' by implicating signs in *bodies* and *images* ('beyond our experience,' farther than the 'image of the Mother—or that of the Father' (Deleuze 1964, 95, 92, 67–68, and 80–81on homosexuality as the 'truth of love'). Whence our thesis: it is Masoch who immerses *for real* (*pour de vrai*) the philosopher Deleuze *in* 'literature' (whence the obligatory quote marks—see the citation from Wanda used here as an epigraph—once literature passes into the 'impersonal' of a logic of sensation). This 'literature' is placed here under the sign of 'minorities' *and* of the contestation of the 'inflation of the father' in 'Freudian psychoanalysis,' to which it opposes: (1) the symptomatology at work in Masoch—knowing that "love, according to him, is not separable from a cultural, political, social and ethnological complex" (pp. 40–42 of the article from 1961); (2) the Jungian symbolic (*la symbolique*) inasmuch as the latter, on the basis of the question of psychosis, combats the image of the father in the Oedipus complex (see the final note 'On Freud and Jung,' p. 46, and Kerslake 2004, 135–157). As for the work by Deleuze and Guattari entitled *Kafka: Toward a Minor Literature*, it was published in 1975 and 'presents' itself as a veritable midway point (*mi-lieu*) between the *Anti-Oedipus* (see Ch. 2: 'A Too Big Oedipus'), from 1972, and *A Thousand Plateaus* (see Kafka's Ch. 9: 'What Is an Assemblage'), released in 1980. Let us signal finally that Guattari denounced very early on the 'Heideggerian tendency' – 'One ends up with Heidegger's philosophy' – of a psychoanalysis for which the unconscious is 'structured like a language', see for example « Introduction à la psychothérapie institutionnelle » (1962-3), in F. Guattari, *Psychanalyse et transversalité*, Paris, François Maspero, 1972, p. 47-51.

[67] This is the conclusion of Foucault's article on Blanchot, 'La pensée du dehors' ('The thought of the outside'), *Critique* 229 (June 1966), reprinted in Foucault 1994.

[68] The quotation from G. Bateson is extracted from Bateson 1977, 113.

This limit-experimentation of a pure immanence, we are told, is inevitable under the practical formula of the BwO—for it is the Body without Organs in which the formal identity of the self [moi] is lost with the substantial integrity of the body in an (anti)logic of sensation. So that the declaration of war of Artaud the Schizo, in To Have Done with the Judgment of God, *against God-the-Father and his power of infinitely* organising *exclusions through his mastery of the disjunctive syllogism, will proceed from the maso body which* suspends *(orgasm, division) and gets itself suspended in order to halt the regulated, designated exercise of organs, an exercise that the Father's coercion partakes in:* "For you can tie me up if you want to, but there is nothing more useless than an organ"(Deleuze & Guattari 1980, 150).[69] *If you want to?* Cruelty *of Artaud against the fake simplicity of language, when its first function is that of* giver of orders *(obeying and making one obey the Father who subtends all speech (langue): the* rection). *Artaud, Masoch, Hölderlin… Lived Things* [Choses vécues (original French title of this Masoch's short story first published in *Revue Bleue*, 1888-1889-1890)] *in the name of the father* when, 'pronouncing the law, he knots together in a major experience space, the rule and language'. *The* Knot *[Nœud] of the Father, 'the word whose first form is that of constraint'* (Foucault, in his review of Laplanche's book, *Hölderlin et la question du père*[70]).

* * *

"I tell myself that it is not a coincidence if Michel [Foucault] emphasizes Sade, and I, on the contrary, Masoch" (Deleuze 1977a, 131).[71] For Deleuze everything essential can be deduced from this. It makes it possible to understand—upstream, as it were—the political community he shares with Foucault: far from being a separate sphere, politics is not only immanent to the entire social field but ontologically constitutive in its difference from ideology—so that politics will everywhere be at the border between the 'micro' and the 'macro,' the 'molecular' and the 'molar.' A border exemplified by Sade *and* Masoch in a

---

[69] This declaration by Artaud is at the heart of the sixth Plateau, 'November 28, 1947 – How to Make Oneself a Body without Organs?' which never stops eliciting the return of the masochist as the constructor of immanence. As for the identity 'Body without Organs': 'Body without Orgasm' has been registered by Michel 2003, 464. Artaud, once again, in a text from May 1947 entitled *The Human Body*: '[...] the coitus of sexuality has been engendered only to make the body forget, through the erythrism of orgasm, that it is a bomb, a magnetized torpedo [...]' (Artaud 1947, 1518). Finally, Lacan: 'This place of the God-the-Father, it is the one that I have designated as the Name-of-the-Father ...' (J. Lacan, 'La méprise du sujet supposé savoir,' in Lacan 1968, 39). In this regard, we cannot but refer now to the indispensable flattening out of the Lacanian New Testament proposed by M. Tort (2005).

[70] M. Foucault, « Le 'non' du père » (1962), repris dans Id., *Dits et écrits*, t. I, op. *cit.*, p. 199.

[71] Deleuze 1994. This letter of Deleuze, addressed to Foucault in 1977 (following the publication of the *The Will to Knowledge*), has been reprinted in *Deux Régimes de fous. Textes et entretiens 1975-1995* (Paris: Minuit, 2003). (Deleuze 2003.)

double parody of the philosophy of history: "an ironic thought, in function of the revolution of '89, [...] a humorous thought, in relation to the revolutions of '48" in the Austrian Empire (Deleuze 1967a, 79–80). And one may then grasp—downstream, as it were—the question disputed by Deleuze and Foucault concerning the primacy of desire or power, which is founded in turn on the deconstruction of the sado-masochist pseudo-unity. Sade *or* Masoch: *either* an ironic thinking of the *objective institution* which takes as its model the anarchic reign of the transgressive father in a paranoid projection that reverses the law, offering, as its derivative truth, pure relations of forces (*rapports de force*) as the truth of power; *or* the *private contract* with the oral mother which annuls the law of the father in the expiation of genital sexuality (there is no *sexual possession* in Masoch) in order to induce the birth of the new man of 'fantastic' desire (absolute *chastity* of these romantic-thriller [*roses-noirs*] novels) and of the solitary woman (a second, parthenogenetic birth). And therefore *a practice, a humoristic diversion [dé-tournement] of the contract, the contract which confers to the woman all the rights in order to withdraw from the* subject *all of his rights* ('wholly absolute renunciation of your self'), *including the right to the name, the subversion of the contract qua bourgeois liberal form of a patriarchal society* (the conjugal contract), *a subversion beyond the purview of transgression.* Celebrated by Foucault in his 'Preface to Transgression,' it is no accident that Bataille is contested by Deleuze as *priestly and French* in his *Dialogues* with Claire Parnet: the Suspensive instead of the Negative. In his 1977 letter to Michel Foucault, published under the title 'Desire and Pleasure,' the primacy of desire (over pleasure *and* power) rests on the processual affirmation of a field of immanence whose reality condition is doubly destructive of the image of the father: through the unbinding of desire from the pleasure that comes to *discharge*, to interrupt from the outside the intensive positivity of desire (desire is no more Nature than it is Transcendence, it is Life *denaturalised*[72] in a *supra- or ultrasensualism*: it is the diversion of Goethe's *Übersinnlichkeit* carried out by Masoch), when Sade instead promoted the force of pleasure against the

---

[72] Foucault's 'Preface to Transgression' opened precisely with this *denaturalisation* that characterises 'modern sexuality,' 'from Sade to Freud' (*Critique* 195–196 [1963], *Hommage à G. Bataille*; reprinted in Foucault 1954-1975, 233-250. The reversal of the Foucauldian 'dispositif' carried out by Deleuze measures up here to the unbinding of desire and literature with regard to death. That is because, from the Deleuzean point of view, in spite of what Foucault might hold (p. 246), one can indeed pass from the 'little death' to the big death and to the immersion of this sexuality in a language without outside (Sade)—unlike Death conceived as this interior limit which causes the failure of the speaking subject in his claim to say it all (*de tout dire*). Had not Sade presented his *Philosophy in the Bedroom* as a 'posthumous work by the author of *Justine*'? See here the article, foundational in every respect, by Blanchot, 'La littérature et le droit à la mort,' in Blanchot 1947.

weakness of desire, through the dis-identification of desire from the Lack that comes to subject it from within to the Law (desire is Out-law [*Hors-la-loi*]). If it is in the same way "that desire is brought under the law of lacking and in line with the norm of pleasure" (Deleuze 1977a, 131)[73], its liberation will be a line of flight out of the *organisations* of the Father-State, starting with this organism of the phallus-man to which the masochist opposes a suffering that neutralises it (by *suspending* the organisation of the organs), undoing its hierarchical organicity (instead of re-organising the hierarchy of bodies on the basis of sex, of the Organ which bears witness to the 'extreme sensibility of organisation') (Sade 1785, 292)[74]: Sade as a 'meticulous anatomist'[75] (Foucault 1975, 820) in order to constitute a 'body without organs.' And, from what Artaud calls 'the anatomical register [*cadastre*] of the present body,' to extract [*dégager*], and to invest [*engager*] the purely intensive plane of consistency of desire. (In a rather Hegelian fashion, the last Foucault will counter this stance through the *use of pleasure*, which must nourish desire in order to trans-form the simplicity of the natural movement of life into the 'spiritual' experience of the subject.[76]) Immanent plane of assemblages in which desire is defined as the process of production whose writing is nourished far from the equilibrium of linguistic constants; a 'literary' war machine *contra* the transcendent plane of organisation which enforces a supplementary dimension from within: against the proto-structuralism of Goethe, 'the greatest representative of major language,' Deleuze poses the becomings of Kleist's Penthesilea or the cliché-characters, devoid of all interiority, of the Anti-German philo-Semitic Masoch.[77] One will no longer be surprised that the intervention

---

[73] In Foucault, on the contrary, the 'counter-attack' against psychoanalysis consists of opposing sex-desire (from which one must free oneself, since it maintains the 'analytic' articulation) with pleasures-bodies 'in their multiplicity and their possibility of resistance' (Foucault 1976, 208).

[74] Sade 1785 / 1986, 292).

[75] This expression appears in an interview by Foucault, 'Sade, sergent du sexe' (*Cinématographe* 16 [Dec. 1975–Jan. 1976]; reprinted in Foucault 1954-1975, 820. In this interview Foucault proposes that Sade formulated 'the eroticism proper to a disciplinary society' – 'so much the worse for the literary beatification of Sade' ... The relentless, sadistic concern with the organ is opposed by the dismantlement of organicity ('the body dis-organises itself,' writes Foucault) associated with the 'slow movements of pleasure-pain,' 'outside all the programmes of desire.' What a singular exchange this is between Foucault and Deleuze: the dis-organisation of bodies is put under the aegis of pleasure in this critique of Sade which reinforces the critique of desire! Misusing the famous sentence from *The Discourse on Language* on Hegel, one would like to say here that Foucault permits us to gauge what is still Sadean in the indictment of his positions.

[76] See Foucault 1984; Foucault 1981–1982.

[77] As R. Michel rightly comments, "he says just as *little* about it as the character acts about it" (p. 459). In his *Autobiography*, Masoch represents himself as the vile little fox of German literature ("exposed to the same persecutions in the coop of German literature"), see

Éric Alliez

aimed at Foucault concludes with the distinction between these 'two very different planes' which will subtend the entire surface of *A Thousand Plateaus*, beginning with its attack on the Book-Form, regarding which it is a question of 'subtracting the uniqueness' proper to the paternal function and to its sublation by the signifier: 'to write at n–1' (Deleuze & Guattari 1980, 6).

'To write at n–1' less in order to promote the more 'patchy,' more 'fragmentary' forms demanded in principle by the new vitalist philosophy (a *biophilosophy*), rather than to pass through the sieve of the most pitiless critique the major language of this Western philosophy in which "the paternal Spirit [...] realised itself in the world qua totality, and in a knowing subject as proprietor" (Deleuze 1989, 86). And, by the same token, to operate—in a clinic of language wherein the invention of new possibilities of life for the missing people is played out—the *transformation of biophilosophy into biopolitics* ('politics and experimentation,' write Deleuze and Guattari). For it is in the world, in the real, that one must learn to heal Life from the Knowledge of the Father and from its *points of reference* [*repères*] which nourish the majoritarian *standard* [*étalon*]—so that life and knowledge are no longer opposed to one another, at the same time as the domination of language [*langue*] over the word [*parole*] in the Text ceases. Between the critical and the clinical, the term Pop-philosophy once meant the following programme of *dephiliation*: to turn thought into a nomad power by writing only in order to trace lines of flight that *construct* the uninterrupted process of desire in the language-bodies of a community of celibate machines, orphans of the father (writing at *n – the father*, as in the famous opening of the *Anti-Oedipus*). It is in this sense that *desiring machines*—the machinic assemblage of desire (= constructivist by 'nature')—bring back the *communism* of Masoch in an *ascesis* (= a suspense crisscrossed by waves) which "has always been the condition of desire" (Deleuze & Parnet 1977b, 74).[78] That is because Masoch is, for Deleuze, the operational sign of the construction of the plane of immanence of desire, when the latter turns into the question of writing, in a becoming-woman of man whose reality condition is a becoming-animal of the one (*Venus in Furs*, who seems to have

---

Sacher Masoch 2004, 130; and 139–141 for the 'critical' anthology collected by the author: a 'Judeo-French' sacrilege against German literature. The translator, Michel-François Demet, recalls that *Die Ideale der Zeit* (1876, translated the following year in French under the title *Les Prussiens d'aujourd'hui* [*The Prussians Today*]) was immediately designated as the most 'anti-German' work imaginable ...

[78] We reencounter in these pages from *Dialogues*, which affirm the constructivism of desire, all the themes of the notes addressed to Foucault, including the question of the 'masochist assemblage' (Deleuze & Parnet 1977b, 74–75). On Masoch's agricultural communism, see Deleuze 1967, 94ff. Very influenced by Bakhunin and the pan-Slav libertarian current, this theme of the 'man of the commune' was already present in the article from 1961.

no other aim than to "wear furs as often as possible, especially when she is behaving cruelly"[79]) (Deleuze 1967a, 277) as well as of the other (*Loup et louve*[80]—but everywhere on the side of the 'victim' in these novels of training in which she who must train/affect is herself trained/affected: it is a 'cycle of forces': "the woman transmits acquired animal forces to the innate forces of man," "woman and animal, animal and man have become indiscernible") (Deleuze 1993, 54)[81]. Deleuze underlines the fact that this relation of man to animal—such as it leads the masochist body to the intensity of a non-organic life as the power to affect *and* to be affected (Masochian immanence) by the forces that it knows how to seize in a *combat-within-the-Self* [*combat-entre-Soi*] which implicates and complicates the whole Outside (Masoch's novels of atmosphere)—"is without doubt what psychoanalysis has constantly ignored, because it sees in it all-too-human Oedipal figures" (Deleuze 1993, 54)[82] ... We can observe, on this basis, Masoch as an effect of announcement: that one will be unable to 'exit philosophy' without, through 'literature and life'[83], exiting psychoanalysis. From the deconstruction of the sado-masochist entity to the annulment of the signifying phallus which is written, how could it not be, Φ: one will also require, from this vantage point, a Re-presentation of Masoch in which it will no longer in any way be possible (*neither* imaginary figures, *nor* symbolic functions) to re-cognize structuralism.[84] For, unlike philosophy, which is to be 'withdrawn' [*sortir*] from its State-Form (the History of philosophy), by restoring its essential relation to non-philosophy (percepts and affects that *force* us to think in an immediate and intensive

---

[79] According to the terms of the *Contrat entre Mme Fanny de Pistor et Leopold de Sacher Masoch* (Deleuze 1967a, 277).

[80] As Deleuze notes, 'In *Loup et louve* the heroine asks her suitor to let himself be sown up in a wolf-skin, to live and howl like a wolf and to let himself be hunted' (Deleuze, 1967a, 94).

[81] Note that the Sadean man-woman (*Juliette*) is immune to any becoming-animal. A fortiori, this is the case for man qua Sadean *type* (of the pervert).

[82] On the 'combat within oneself' [*combat entre Soi*], see Deleuze 1993, 132.

[83] According to the manifesto-title of the first chapter of *Essays Critical and Clinical*.

[84] See Deleuze 1967b, 170–192 (= G. Deleuze, 'A quoi reconnaît-on le structuralisme?' in *Histoire de la philosophie*, vol. VII, ed. F. Châtelet [Paris: Hachette, 1972]). Written in 1967, this article of 'recognition' (in the twofold sense of the term) of Lacanianism is concerned with engaging structure qua 'virtuality.' But here, as Deleuze and Guattari will be obliged to re-cognise a posteriori, it is Milner's proposal which is the right one: 'there is no virtual' or 'the only virtual is imaginary' in a doctrine of the signifier that prolongs itself—as one can read in "How can we recognize Structuralism?"—'in *the complete determination* of singular points' (Deleuze 1967b, 177). Whence Milner's accusation: Deleuze, in this text which is contemporary with *Difference and Repetition* and *Logic of Sense*, will never have been anything other than the philosopher of 'what *doxa* called structuralism' (See Milner 2002, 159, 169). As we know, the critique of structuralism begun with *Anti-Oedipus* is completed in *A Thousand Plateaus*.

relation with the outside), one must withdraw from psychoanalysis *completely*, going beyond a certain ambivalence maintained by the *Anti-Oedipus* with respect to Lacan[85] (this will be the case in *A Thousand Plateaus*), in order to produce for thought—*outside the Father as the Power of judging* and *against the filth-writing* [*l'écriture-cochonnerie*] *of 'Father Being'* [*Père Étant*] *who lacks the entire 'infinite outside'* (Artaud)—wholly other becomings, in a politics of *unnatural* [*contre nature*] assemblages, freed from the infinite debt towards his Name. Because "the real is artifice—and not the impossible, as Lacan says" (Guattari 1970, 210).[86]

* * *

Lacan: the phallus is the "sign in which the logos marks life with its imprint"— and it is in this regard that it "revealed to us its symbolic function: in the castration complex" (Lacan 1958b, 171).[87] *Whence the fact that "the phallus is the imaginary element that symbolises the operation through which the real of life is sacrificed to the Other of language"* (Lacan 1959, 40). *Deleuze: "it is the passage of life within language that constitutes Ideas," as 'excesses of language'* [*écarts de langage*] (Deleuze 1993, 5) *stopping it from giving orders to life (an order from the father to his son ...). It follows that Deleuze does not want to say* writing [*l'écriture*], *this far too 'pure writing' arising 'from a material vacuum,' and separated "from other common languages [...] whose 'noise' might hinder it"* (Barthes 1971, 4)[88]:

---

[85] See Deleuze & Guattari 1972, 53, 83. About the thought of Lacan: "Is it simply a matter of oedipalising the schizo? Or isn't it something else entirely, even the opposite? Schizophrenising, schizophrenising the field of the unconscious, as well as the historical social field, in order to explode the yoke of Oedipus ..." "But [...] Lacan seems to maintain a kind of projection of signifying chains onto a despotic signifier, and to suspend everything from a lacking term, lacking from itself and reintroducing lack into the series of desire, onto which it imposes an exclusive usage. Is it possible to denounce Oedipus as a myth and nevertheless to maintain the castration complex is itself not a myth, but on the contrary something real?" The explanation passes through Guattari's response (at the roundtable organised by *La Quinzaine littéraire*), which opposed the overcoding of the phallic function according to Lacan to the deterritorialisation of the partial object in the *objet petit a* which could contain '*the germ* of the liquidation of the totalitarianism of the signifier' (note the fierce objection of Serge Leclaire in his own reply!), see Deleuze 1967b, 222–224 (= 'Deleuze et Guattari s'expliquent ...' *La Quinzaine littéraire* 143 [June 1972]: 16–30). See also the passage on Lacan ('we hoped to help him schizophrenically ...') at the beginning of the 'Entretien sur *L'Anti-Œdipe*' in Deleuze 1990, 24–25 (= *L'Arc* 49 [1972]), whose genesis we can now follow in Guattari's *Écrits pour L'Anti-Œdipe* (Guattari 2004), a collection of letters and notes sent to Deleuze.

[86] Guattari 2004, 210, dated 01/10/70. Guattari's entire research plan can be read in these lines: "The fusion of the most artificial modernism and of the naturing nature of desire" (2004, 147, dated 28/04/70).

[87] In the guise of a response to these people who "resent our invoking Freud, and to miss the essential, by reducing to the field of speech and language [...] a movement of being which subtends and exceeds it on all sides" (Lacan 1958b, 171).

[88] Read a little further on for the introduction of the Lacanian reference.

it is the 'problem of writing [écrire],' of 'becoming something other than a writer' which opens Essays Critical and Clinical.[89] *Writing [l'écrire] is driven by no other necessity than that of taking language in its entirety to its limit, to its outside 'beyond all syntax,' to its point of suspension in the 'stammering' of language, carrying the outside inside, "as if the language were becoming animal"* (Deleuze 1993, 55),[90] *an(ti)-Oedipal pack-animal, incestuous animality ex-posed to the Thing prior to words whose Vision de-structures, dis-identifies the speaking-subject in order to free life wherever it is the prisoner of 'logos.' Antilogos*[91] *developing into Anti-structure, the* Anti-Oedipus*, with its cohort of 'novelists,' is an anti-phallogocentric war machine. And if the Artaudian control of this machine has been noted elsewhere, once the Body without Organs dis-organised the* Logic of Sense[92] *(this book, Deleuze prefaced, is 'an* attempt *at a logical and psychoanalytic novel'), and we have underlined here the Masochian re-presentation of Artaud in* A Thousand Plateaus*, we can now remark the presence throughout the work of Deleuze of the fractured line of Masoch's body-language: because "sexual organisation is a prefiguration of the organisation of language"* (Deleuze 1969, 241–242), *it is the suspense of bodies—masochistically dis-organised and erogenised ('a properly masochist "erogeneousness"') in a delirious formation whose 'perversion' into masculine-feminine is not familial but world-historical (the complementarity of contract and infinite suspense is* post-Kantian*)—which has made to stammer the language of the father, which is called 'maternal' to inscribe more intimately the master-signifier of Oedipus into the chains of the linguistic order.*[93] *Everywhere*

---

[89] These themes are already present in *Dialogues* (Deleuze & Parnet 1977b, 32–34). The famous Barthesian distinction between *écrivain* and *écrivant* is reversed as a function of the argumentation used to ground it. As a reminder: 'The *écrivain* partakes of the priest, the *écrivant* of the clerk; the word of the one is an intransitive act [...], the word of the other is an activity' (Barthes 1964, 157). It follows that, for Deleuze, 'Bartleby is not a metaphor of the writer'—according to the first sentence of 'Bartleby, or the Formula' (Deleuze 1989, 68).

[90] G. Deleuze, 'Re-présentation de Masoch,' in Deleuze 1993, 73. Deleuze borrows here the key expression of Pascal Quignard in *L'être du balbutiement. Essai sur Sacher Masoch* (Quignard 1969).

[91] 'Antilogos' is the title of the first chapter of the second part ('The Literary Machine') added by Deleuze to the first edition of *Proust and Signs* (1970/1976). The conclusion ('Presence and Function of Madness: The Spider'), reprinted and modified from an article published in 1973, unveils the narrator of the *Recherche* as 'an enormous Body without organs' whose truth is universal schizophrenia.

[92] See Alliez 2004a; Alliez 2004b. (An expanded version of this article has since been published in the edited volume *Deleuze and the Social*.)

[93] See Lacan, *Les non dupes errent*, 19 March 1974 (unpublished): "The mother, through whom the word is transmitted, the mother, we must say, is reduced to translate it, this name [*nom*] [of the father] to translate it by a no [*non*], precisely the no said by the father ..." (to the enjoyment of the mother). According to Assoun's effective summary in his *Lacan* (Assoun 2003), the homophonic parody of the *Nom du père*, Name of the Father, in *non dupes errant*, the non-dupes err, signifies that the psychotic would be the one who does not manage to turn

in Deleuze, we will hazard saying, Masoch is caught up in the changing of the function of language, which no longer expresses anything but intensities, in the asignifying *intensive usage of language as a 'linguistic' construction of immanence. That is because the superiority of American literature and its writers*—"traitor to one's own reign, traitor to one's sex, to one's class, to one's majority" (Deleuze & Parnet 1977b, 33) ... *is unimpeachable when it is a matter of making a* 'psychotic breath' *pass through the regularity of language.* "The American is the one who has freed himself from the English paternal function, he is the son of a torn father, of all nations" and who only believes in a 'society without fathers'... Here lies "the schizophrenic vocation of American literature" (Deleuze 1989, 84–85).[94]

The Legacy of Cain *(according to the great cycle outlined by Masoch), of wandering [*errance*] that frees fraternity between men from the* philiation *of the father, the resemblance of the father in the son abolished together with both origin and transcendence by means of the fabulating function of a self which "is* 'corrupted' *only because, in the first instance, it is dissolved'* (Deleuze 1969, 283), *dis-location of the subject and dis-locution of thought, drawing the 'community of the celibate' into the unlimited becoming of a world in process ... Now, this Masoch, who has departed from the Text for the sake of an Experimentation-Life, is a* political programme *that Deleuze throws at us, since "the only real danger is the return of the father"* (Deleuze 1989, 88). *(Of the father, Lacan would persevere:* 'inasmuch as his name is the vector of an incarnation of Law in desire'.[95]*) We should pick up from here, from the Deleuzo-Masochian knot of literary clinic and critique of psychoanalysis, the much disputed question of a 'Deleuzean politics.' And it should not displease to take up again this urgent question*, with Guattari, *because it is also the Masochian line that precipitates the encounter – not without the latter being* politically *precipitated by the former.*

* * *

Translated by Alberto Toscano

Bibliography

Alliez, É. 2004a. '"The Body without Organs"—Condition, or, The Politics of Sensation.' In *Discern(e)ments. Deleuzian Aesthetics / Esthétiques deleuziennes*. Edited

---

himself into a dupe, the 'good dupe' of the signifier (p. 53) ... The one who does not manage to introduce the good distance with respect to the Thing (the archaic Mother targeted by incest), a distance that would condition the very existence of the speaking subject.

[94] 'To introduce a bit of psychosis into English neurosis' (Deleuze 1989, 72).
[95] J. Lacan, « Note sur l'enfant » (octobre 1969), in Id., *Autres écrits*, Paris, Éd. du Seuil, 2001, p. 373.

by J. de Bloois, S. Houppermans, F.-W. Korsten. Amsterdam and New York: Éditions Rodopi, 2004, pp. 93-113.

———. 2004b. 'Anti-oedipus—Thirty Years On.' *Radical Philosophy* 204 (March 2004).

———. 2006. "*Anti-Œdipus*—Thirty Years On (Between Art and Politics). In *Deleuze and the Social*. Edited by M. Fugslang and B.M. Sorensen. Edinburgh: Edinburgh University Press, 2006, pp. 151-168.

Artaud, A. 1947. 'Le corps humain.' In *Œuvres*. Edited by E. Grossman. Paris: Gallimard, 2004.

Assoun, P.-L. 2003. *Lacan*. Paris: PUF, 2003.

Barthes, R. 1964. 'Écrivains et écrivants.' In *Essais critiques*. Paris: Le Seuil, 1964, pp. 147-154.

———. 1971. *Sade, Fourier, Loyola*. Translated by R. Miller. Berkeley and Los Angeles: University of California Press, 1976.

Bateson, G. 1977. *Steps to an Ecology of Mind*. Chicago: University of Chicago Press, 2000.

Blanchot, M. 1947. 'La littérature et le droit à la mort.' In *La Part du feu*. Paris: Gallimard, 1947, 291-331.

Deleuze, G. 1964. *Proust and Signs*. Translated by R. Howard. London: Athlone, 2000.

———. 1967a. 'Coldness and Cruelty.' In *Masochism*. Translated by J. McNeil. New York: Zone Books, 1989, pp. 9-138.

———. 1967b. 'How do We Recognize Structuralism?' In *Desert Islands and Other Texts, 1953–1974*. Edited by D. Lapoujade. Translated by M. Taormina. London: MIT Press, 2004, pp. 170-192.

———. 1969. *The Logic of Sense*. Translated by M. Lester and C. Stivale. Edited by C. V. Bounderas. London: Athlone, 1990.

———. 1977a. 'Desire and Pleasure.' In *Two Regimes of Madness: Texts and Interviews, 1975–1995*. Edited by D. Lapoujade. Translated by A. Hodges and M. Taormina. Cambridge, MA and London: MIT Press, 2006.

———. 1989. 'Bartleby; or, The Formula.' In *Critical and Clinical*. Translated by D. W. Smith. London: Verso, 1998, pp. 68-90.

———. 1990. *Pourparlers*. Paris: Les Éditions de Minuit, 1990.

———. 1993. *Essays Critical and Clinical*. Translated by D. W. Smith. London: Verso, 1998.

———. 1994. 'Désir et plaisir.' *Magazine littéraire* 325 (1994), pp. 57-65.

———. 2003. *Two Regimes of Madness: Texts and Interviews 1975–1995*. Edited by D. Lapoujade. Translated by A. Hodges and M. Taormina. Cambridge, MA and London: MIT Press, 2006.

Deleuze, G., and C. Bene. 1979. *Superpositions*. Paris: Les Éditions de Minuit, 1979.

Deleuze, G., and C. Parnet. 1977b. *Dialogues*. Translated by H. Tomlinson and B. Habberjam. New York: Columbia University Press, 1987.

Deleuze, G., and F. Guattari. 1972. *Anti-Oedipus: Capitalism and Schizophrenia*.

Translated by R. Hurley, M. Seem and H. R. Lane. Minneapolis: University of Minnesota Press, 1983.

———. 1975. *Kafka, Pour une littérature mineure*. Paris: Éditions de Minuit, 1975.

———. 1980. *A Thousand Plateaus: Capitalism and Schizophrenia*. Translated by B. Massumi. London: Athlone, 1988.

Foucault, M. 1954-1975. *Dits et Ecrits I*.

1966. 'Michel Foucault, Blanchot—The Thought from Outside.' In *Foucault/Blanchot*. Translated by B. Massumi. New York: Zone Books, 1987.

———. 1975. 'Sade, Sergent du sexe.' In *Dits et Écrits II, 1970–1975*. Edited by D. Defert and F. Ewald. Paris: Gallimard, 1994.

———.1976. *La volonté de savoir*. Paris: Gallimard, 1976.

———. 1981–1982. *L'herméneutique du sujet*. Cours au Collège de France, 1981–1982. Paris: Gallimard, 2001.

———.1984. *L'usage des plaisirs*. Paris: Gallimard, 1984.

Guattari, F. 2004. *Écrits pour L'Anti-Œdipe*. Paris: Éd. Lignes – Manifestes, 2004.

Kerslake, C. 2004. 'Rebirth through Incest. On Deleuze's Early Jungianism.' *Angelaki* 9, no. 1 (2004), pp. 135-157.

Lacan, J. 1958a. *Le Séminaire, Livre V, 1957–1958: Les formations de l'inconscient*. Paris: Le Seuil, 1998.

———. 1958b. 'La psychanalyse vraie, et la fausse.' In *Autres Écrits*. Paris: Le Seuil, 2001.

———. 1959. *Séminaire VI: Le désir et son interprétation*. Paris: Navarin, 1959.

———. 1963. 'Kant avec Sade.' In D. A. F. de Sade. *Oeuvres complètes*. Paris: Pauvert, 1986–1991.

———. 1966. 'In Memory of Ernest Jones: On His Theory of Symbolism.' In *Écrits*. Translated by B. Fink and R. Grigg. New York and London: Norton, 2002, pp. 697-717.

———. 1968. 'La méprise du sujet supposé savoir.' In *Scilicet I*. Paris: Le Seuil, 1968.

———.'Les non dupes errent.' Unpublished.

Laplanche, J. 1961. *Hölderlin et la question du père*. Paris: PUF, 1961.

Michel, R. 2003. 'Der Anti-Masoch. Essay über die irrungen der maso (miso) analyse.' In *Phantom der Lust. Visionen des Masochismus*. Vol. I. Edited by P. Weibel. Graz: Neue Galerie Graz am Landesmuseum Joanneum, 2003.

Milner, J.-C. 2002. *Le périple structural. Figures et paradigme*. Paris: Le Seuil, 2002.

Quignard, P. 1969. *L'Être du balbutiement. Essai sur Sacher Masoch*. Paris: Mercure de France, 1969.

Sacher Masoch, L. von. 1876-1886. *Écrits autobiographiques et autres textes*. Paris: Éditions Léo Schreer, 2004.

Sacher Masoch, W. von. 1906/1908. *Meine Lebensbeichte. Masochismus & Masochisten*. Munich: Belleville, 2003.

Sade, D. A. F. de. 1785. 'Les cent vingt journées de Sodome.' In *Oeuvres Complètes*. Paris: Pauvert, 1986.

Tort, M. 2005. *Fin du dogme paternel* II, 2. Paris: Aubier, 2005.

Deleuze's Passive Syntheses of Time and the Dissolved Self

Leen De Bolle

In *Difference and Repetition* (1968) Deleuze elaborates a highly paradoxical notion of subjectivity. He proposes a notion of the self that is not defined by a unity of apperception, a substantial essence, nor a constituting consciousness, but a dissolved self. The dissolved self opens up on to an impersonal repetition, a flow of neutralised energy that consists in a plurality of disjunctive series of intensities which have nothing to do with contradiction or opposition. Repetition becomes the automatic movement of the event that constantly produces differences. This is the object of a radical vitalism in which Deleuze does not deny the dark or the destructive, the cruel and brute forces of life. He states that all the forces of life have to be lived through and affirmed as an endless repetition in which the person has dissolved. Like Nietzsche, he proposes a philosophy in which all negative or reactive forces are eliminated in favour of a creative energy which happens in spite of the person, as an automatic repetition that proceeds in an auto-production of difference.

This radical affirmation is a counter-intuitive and stubborn intuition out of which arise a lot of difficulties and questions. But this vitalism does not remain a vague intuition or an arbitrary opinion. Deleuze elaborates his intuition in respect to the history of philosophy. He pursues long discussions with a variety of philosophers, scientists, writers, poets, artists … by means of which he constructs his own plane of consistency in which this vitalist intuition becomes a consistent theory of being. Deleuze's vitalist intuition is presented (in the earlier works) as an ontology of the virtual, but at the same time it is a practice, a 'way of life.' Although Deleuze elaborates his intuition by means of a very sophisticated conceptual framework (especially in the earlier works, the monographs, *Difference and Repetition* and *The Logic of Sense*), he never proposes his vitalist intuition as an abstract idea but, on the contrary, he always presents it as a matter of concrete encounter, of real experience. This fits in his methodological assumption of what he calls 'transcendental casuistry.' No external principles or laws condition the forces of life, but every singular case contains its own conditions. As such, philosophizing requires constantly new encounters with concrete 'cases.' This implies a radical and highly paradoxical dissolution of the self in favour of a philosophy of the 'pure event.'

A concrete example of such a dissolution of the self is the Andalusian celebration of life and death, of history and future, of heaven and earth. Although Deleuze himself does not refer to it, the flamenco can produce a state of mind in which all forces of life are affirmed and in which all negative and reactive forces are overcome: the *duende*. The *duende* is a 'mysterious force' whose experience Goethe believed everyone could partake in, but which has never been explained by any philosopher (García Lorca 1933, 3). The *duende* cannot be explained, it cannot be understood, and yet, the phenomenon is known everywhere in Andalusia and people there recognize it instinctively. According to García Lorca, the *duende* is a dark and impersonal force that flows through the person, at which point all activity and willpower are relinquished. García Lorca writes:

> The *duende* is a force, not a labour, a struggle not a thought [...] it is not a question of skill, but of a style that's truly alive [...]. The *duende* is not in the throat: the *duende* surges up, inside, from the soles of the feet. Meaning it's not a question of skill, but of a style that's truly alive: meaning it's in the veins: meaning, it's of the most ancient culture of immediate creation. (García Lorca 1933, 5)

With this intuition in mind, we will examine how the dissolution of the self must be understood, and how this dissolution can paradoxically lead towards novelty and creativity. Although the *duende* is a concrete experience, we will try to place this phenomenon in the broader theoretical framework of Deleuze's dissolution of the self as he elaborates it in *Difference and Repetition*.

The paradox of a dissolved self in *Difference and Repetition* functions as the condition for Deleuze's later works. He will then speak in terms of productive machines, schizophrenic disjunctions, impersonal becomings, rhizome, ritornello, the infinitive verb, the fourth person singular, homo tantum, eventum tantum, 'a' life (with the indefinite article 'a'). With his theory of the dissolved self, Deleuze opposes a nomadic philosophy to the hegemony of representational thinking. The latter he calls a sedentary thinking that operates by means of the categories of identity, resemblance, analogy, and opposition. These categories constitute the principle of sufficient reason, or the foundation from which the 'I think' conceives reality. The nomadic philosophy that Deleuze wants to elaborate consists in a thinking without ground: a groundless thinking in which everything happens in the middle [*au milieu*] without a beginning or an end: "What matters on a path, what matters on a line, is always the middle, not the beginning or the end. We are always in the middle of a path, in the middle of something" (Deleuze & Parnet 1977, 21–22).

With this nomadic thinking, Deleuze wants to initiate a new image of thought, a thought of the concrete, of the affect, of corporal encounter as well as of an ascetic minimalism: a discharge of all (empirical) contents. This nomadic image of thought implies a radical openness to the unexpected, the non-representative, the unthinkable, the radically new ... The nomad is indeed the person *par excellence* who encounters the new. In his travelling he leaves behind all acquired convictions and identifications. The nomad discharges himself to become empty and to travel on without roots, memories, or burdens. In this nomadic thought that finds its most heterogeneous and extreme articulations throughout Deleuze's entire *oeuvre*, the notion of the dissolved self as a system of three passive syntheses forms the core of his argumentation

1. The passive synthesis as a transcendental field of the unconscious

Deleuze describes his dissolved self as a triple structure of passive syntheses by means of which he wants to re-invent the project of a transcendental philosophy. He opposes his system of the three syntheses to Kant's architecture of the three Critiques. Deleuze's three syntheses of time, in which he elaborates the respective conditions for the present, the past, and the future, can be considered the counterparts of Kant's syntheses of sensibility, understanding, and reason. As Kant proposes in each synthesis one faculty which is legislative over the others, and which provides the other faculties with their proper function within the constellation, Deleuze attributes to each respective synthesis the status of present, past, or future reality. At the level of the first synthesis, only the present is real. Past and future are mere dimensions or functions of the present. In the second synthesis only the past is real, and present and future are mere functions of it. Finally, in the third synthesis, only the future is real, and past and present are mere functions of the future.

With the system of the passive syntheses, Deleuze starts the construction of his own transcendental philosophy. This new transcendental philosophy does not culminate in representation by recognition, or the faculty of the understanding that connects the objects with a thinking subject by the use of concepts, as it did for Kant. Deleuze wants to lead his three syntheses into the play of difference and repetition. These are the transcendental conditions of life in all its aspects. In these dynamics, the notions of difference and repetition get a positive meaning. In representational thinking, difference and repetition were commonly understood in a negative sense: repetition was always a function of identity as the repetition of the same, while difference stood for that which did not belong to the identity of a concept. In Deleuze's system, the three syntheses of time are three fundamental repetitions, in which the notions of difference and repetition have a fully autonomous and positive meaning.

Deleuze's own transcendental system offers a totally different conception of time and space from Kant's system, where time and space are the formal frames of intuition. Instead of a homogeneous time and space, Deleuze follows Bergson's theory of the notion of intensity and the internally qualitative differences that are distinguished from quantitative or gradual differences. The qualitative differences are differences in nature, while the gradual differences are mere quantities on a numerical scale. In this respect, time and space appear as internally and qualitatively differentiated realities. By distinguishing differences in nature from gradual differences, Bergson wants to deprive time of every quantitative characterisation. The duration that he opposes to the homogeneous frameworks of experience in Kant's transcendental aesthetics constantly grows and changes in quality, without changing in quantity.

Deleuze, however, does not totally disapprove of the Kantian transcendental philosophy. To him, "of all philosophers, Kant is the one who discovers the prodigious domain of the transcendental" (Deleuze 1968, 135). But, instead of retrieving the transcendental conditions of all *possible* experience, Deleuze wants to discover the conditions of *real* experience. Whereas Kant thought of time and space in minimal conditions, Deleuze's conditions of experience are as large and as rich as the real. This fits into a theory of internal genesis instead of external conditioning. Deleuze criticizes the concept of 'possible experience' upon which Kant's transcendental philosophy is based:

> But by whatever manner one defines form, it is an odd procedure since it involves rising from the conditioned to the condition, in order to think of the condition as the simple possibility of the conditioned. Here one rises to a foundation, but that which is founded remains what it was, independently of the operation which founded it [,] and unaffected by it. (Deleuze 1969, 18)

Deleuze relies on Maimon's re-interpretation of Kant to state that Kant's conditions of possible experience are not capable of affecting the real experience. This impossibility is owing to the fact that Kant has conceived intuition and understanding as 'two completely separate sources of knowledge' (Maimon 1790, 40). To overcome this difference in nature, Maimon adds to the transcendental philosophy of Kant a Leibnizian element: the small perceptions. With the notion of small perceptions, Leibniz states, against Locke, that the mind always thinks, but that it is not always conscious of its thoughts. There is a multitude of unconscious perceptions that Leibniz calls 'small perceptions.' Thousands of small perceptions can be integrated into a global, conscious thought: the apperception. According to Leibniz, I can, for example, have a global, conscious apperception of the roaring noise of the sea when I am standing at the shore. But this global apperception is constituted by thousands of unconscious, small perceptions: the perceptions of each wave or drop of water that constitute a continuous variation: "To hear this noise as we do, we must hear the parts which make up this whole, that is the noise of each wave, although each of these little noises makes itself known only when combined confusedly with all the others, and would not be noticed if the wave which made it were by itself" (Leibniz 1704, 54–55). The small perceptions represent a part of the mind that is not enlightened by consciousness: a dark, obscure depth of the mind. As such, the Cartesian 'clear and distinct' ideas are replaced by ideas that are *distinct-obscur*, or, as Deleuze calls it: differential or virtual ideas that contain a variety of different series consisting of embryonic, germinal elements, ordinary series of small perceptions and singular points that are the points of communication between different series.

By this theory of the small perceptions and differential ideas and with the intervention of Maimon's transcendental philosophy, the transcendental unity of Kant's apperception is split up into an unconscious transcendental field that is internally differentiated and that delivers the conditions of the real experience. Deleuze qualifies this mechanism as *transcendental empiricism*. It is in this perspective that the three syntheses of time should be understood. They constitute an unconscious transcendental field. They are three fundamental repetitions of the unconscious that contain the conditions of real experience, as they are as large and as rich as life itself.

Although Deleuze develops with his passive synthesis of time a totally different conception of time than Kant, he appreciates the fact that Kant has introduced the form of time into philosophy. This introduction of time brings Kant to a doubling of the subject. On the one hand, there is an actively thinking transcendental subject, and on the other hand there is a passive, empirical subject, a finite subject that is situated in time and that transforms itself in every becoming as it is constituted by the fact that it is constantly affected. But in the end, Deleuze regrets that Kant has not remained loyal to the consequences of his discovery. He did not think through the idea of a split subject in which the empirical self is irreducible to the transcendental unity of apperception. Kant's transcendental philosophy culminates again into the active cogito. With the Critique of Practical Reason, we assist with the 'resurrection' of God and the I. Moreover, Kant has interpreted the notion of passivity in a restricted way. He has understood passivity as mere receptivity, as a faculty to receive empirical impressions. As such, no passive synthesis is possible in Kant:

> It is true that Kant did not pursue the initiative: both God and the I underwent a practical resurrection. Even in the speculative domain, the fracture is quickly filled by a new form of identity—namely, active synthetic identity; whereas the passive self is defined only by receptivity and, as such, endowed with no power of synthesis. (Deleuze 1968, 87)

For Deleuze, on the contrary, the concept of passivity implies an activity that he calls—according to Plotinus and Hume—contemplation and contraction. But this activity is not initiated by the mind, it is an activity that is a contraction *of the mind*. With the notions of contemplation and contraction, subjective feelings like pain and pleasure are also considered in the passive synthesis. The pleasure principle that Deleuze locates in the synthesis of time will bring him to a confrontation with psychoanalysis and especially with Freud. Deleuze wants to think of a dissolution of the self that is not in conflict with the pleasure principle. In order to provide an alternative for the pathological figures of the dissolution of the self, Deleuze pursues a long and persistent discussion with Freud. He never abandons this difficult, paradoxical thought: the dissolution of the self is a positive, glorious event that needs to be affirmed. Although he uses notions such as desexualisation, masochism, perversion, death instinct, and schizophrenic becomings, his philosophy is always a philosophy of affirmation and creativity. Let us have a closer look at the three syntheses of time to find out how Deleuze can combine an affirmative philosophy with a dissolution of the self.

2. *The first synthesis of time*

The first repetition that constitutes the living present Deleuze calls *habitus*. When the same phenomena occur repeatedly, a difference in the mind is effectuated. The same cases are contracted by the mind in the sense of contemplations. Contemplation means that a synthesis is constituted by elements that are not centralised in the mind. The contemplations are relations exterior to their terms. The syntheses they bring about are passive since "it is not carried out by the mind, but occurs in the mind which contemplates, prior to all memory and reflection" (Deleuze 1968, 71). Following Hume, Deleuze states that contemplation is linked to principles of association such as contiguity, resemblance, and causality that provoke a certain liveliness.

By this liveliness, the experience transgresses itself towards a conviction, an expectation, a habit. As such, the mind becomes a human nature. This human nature is thus constituted without any transcendental operations, nor does it consist of different faculties that differ in nature.

Following Plotinus, Deleuze conceives of contemplation as a contraction which not only concerns perceptive syntheses as in Hume, but which constitutes organic life in a more fundamental way. In this sense, contemplation is not just about habits that we *have*, but about habits that we *are*. The constituting parts of our individuality are, even before we have a perception of them, contractions, fusions of thousands of elements:

> We are made of contracted water, earth, light and air—not merely prior to the recognition or representation of these, but prior to their being sensed. Every organism, in its receptive and perceptual elements, but also in its viscera, is a sum of contractions, of retentions and expectations. (Deleuze 1968, 73)

This metaphysical, Plotinian conception of contemplation enables Deleuze to think about the self without any intervention of consciousness, be it in the sense of a transcendental unity of apperception or of the phenomenological intentional consciousness. As all things are constituted by the light of the One in Plotinus' system, the contemplations that constitute the organic are for Deleuze not *a light shed on the surrounding elements*. They are contractions of *the light that the elements are*. Deleuze asks: "What organism is not made of elements and cases of repetition, of contemplated and contracted water, nitrogen, carbon, chlorides and sulphates, thereby intertwining all the habits of which it is composed?" (Deleuze 1968, 75).

Furthermore, Deleuze says that every contraction constitutes a self, but a partial self, an embryonic, passive self that is constituted by being affected and that transforms itself in every affection. This partial self Deleuze calls a larval subject. The larval subjects always exist in the plural. There are as many larval subjects as there are contractions. This means that the passive synthesis always exists in the plural. The larval selves are not yet a global, conscious self, they are the prefiguration of the individual. At this level, they are characterised by an elementary narcissistic pleasure, by a primary self-fulfilment. As the lower part of the soul in Plotinus fulfils itself with an image of itself by contracting matter, the many larval subjects fulfil themselves with an image of themselves in a contemplation of something else. By their existence alone, the larval subjects are immediately fulfilled with a positive desire. In a Spinozist sense, we could say that their essence is their desire:

> There is a beatitude associated with passive synthesis, and we are all Narcissus in virtue of the pleasure (auto-satisfaction) we experience in contemplating, even though we contemplate things quite apart from ourselves. (Deleuze 1968, 74).

The larval subjects form a pre-individual field of unconscious contractions and contemplations in which desire connects differences in intensity. Deleuze compares this pre-individual field with the Id of Freud. He defines the Id as "a field of individuation in which differences in intensity are distributed here and there in the form of excitations" and as "a mobile distribution of differences and local resolutions within an intensive field" (Deleuze 1968, 96). Deleuze emphasizes that the pleasure that, according to Freud, governs the Id must be understood as a 'principle.' This principle transcends empirical pleasure. It is necessary that the chaotic flow of energy of the Id becomes bound by a principle. The local integrations of these chaotic, disparate excitations are precisely the larval subjects. The pleasure principle stands for the condition under which pleasure becomes bound. This condition is, for Deleuze, the same as the transcendence of experience in Hume's theory of human nature, namely habit. Habit makes pleasure-finding 'a trace': "Habit in the form of a passive binding synthesis precedes the pleasure principle and renders it possible" (Deleuze 1968, 97).

With this first synthesis, however, nothing has been said yet about the global self of consciousness. The development of this global self is involved in a complex structure of two series that are separated from the Id and that continue to proceed in their own ways: the series of the pleasure principle and the series of reality with the demands of conscience and the limitations of reality that restrict the pleasure principle.

Also, the first synthesis cannot contain itself. The living present is always intra-temporal. It ceases to be because of a 'fatigue'[96] of the contemplations. When they become supersaturated, the contractions release and the present moment fades out. At the same time, dreams, imaginary projections, hallucinations, memories populate the mind. The first synthesis cannot explain the passing of the present into the past or the imaginary. It transgresses itself towards a second synthesis in which there is a double development. On the one hand, there is the continuation of the passive synthesis towards the

---

[96] The notion of 'fatigue' allows Deleuze to think of need and the desire that accompanies it to fulfil the need, in a positive sense without any recourse to lack or negativity. Need and desire only originate with the contractions of a contemplating mind. But as long as one contemplates, the need is always fulfilled. Every contraction is a primary satisfaction, an elementary joy. In the contractions, desire is always positive; outside of the contractions, there is no desire. The lack and the negativity only appear on the level of the active synthesis.

past, which constitutes an erotic memory invested by the pleasure principle. On the other hand, there is the series of an active synthesis of memory in a psychological sense that makes recognition, reflection, and representation possible, or the categories that correspond to the reality principle.

3. The second synthesis of time

Of the two series that evolve out of the first synthesis, Deleuze considers the development into the deeper, passive synthesis of memory most fundamental. Next to the fact that this second, passive synthesis is the condition that makes the present pass by, it is also the condition of the active psychological memory. Deleuze uses Bergson's theory of memory as developed in *Matter and Memory* and in *Mind-Energy* to establish a difference in nature between the active memory—this is the psychological memory that makes recognition, reflection and representation possible—and the passive memory. The latter he calls, with Bergson, a pure or virtual memory that opens up onto a pure or virtual past. On the level of the first synthesis, Deleuze also mentions the notion of the past, but this past is only a dimension of the present. Reminiscence is, at this level, the mere representation of an ancient present. The virtual memory, on the contrary, breaks with the chronological succession of moments according to which the past is constituted after the present. The pure past cannot be constituted *after it was present*. This would reduce the past to the shadow of an ancient present. The dreams, hallucinations, and imaginary projections that snatch the self away from the living present and that constantly effectuate deterritorialisations of the actual life are, according to Bergson, constituted *at the same time* as the present moment. Present and past differ in nature, but they coexist as two different worlds. The present concerns the sensory-motor prolongation of bodily movements in a materialistic universe. The pure past, however, stands for a dimension that has released every bond to the materialistic universe. It is non-extensive, spiritual, and virtual. This virtual memory is constituted by a paradoxical mechanism of the de-doubling of every present moment. Every moment splits into two: the present moment and the recollection of that moment, but the recollection happens at the same time as the present moment. Every moment is at the same time perception and recollection, actual and virtual, or, as Bergson formulates it:

> The memory will be seen to duplicate the perception at every moment, to arise with it, to be developed at the same time, and to survive it precisely because it is of a quite different nature. (Bergson 1919, 134)

As such, the past stands for a completely different dimension, which is independent of the actual representation and which becomes invested with desire. This is the fundamental connection of the second synthesis, the marriage of Eros and Mnemosynè: "Eros tears virtual objects [fantasies, dreams, hallucinations ...] out of the pure past and gives them to us in order that they may be lived" (Deleuze 1968, 102–103). The past has released all subordination to the world of representation, the dimension of the present that is characterised by utility, urgency, and response to the current situation.

The virtual past is a zone of being where time emerges in person. Although it is not representative, out of reach, or unassailable (it is a 'virginal' synthesis), the virtual memory accompanies every moment as a character accompanies the person. Following this theory of Bergson's, Deleuze can think through the continuation of the pleasure principle without any conflict with reality. The virtual past differs in nature from the actual present, but at the same time it constitutes, with the actual present, one and the same event.

This idea of the de-doubling of the present moment into actual and virtual series forms the starting point for Deleuze to develop a complete ontology of the virtual. To this Bergsonian idea, Deleuze adds the Leibnizian idea of the small perceptions. The virtual becomes a sub-representative field of individuation that is distinct-obscure. Every object, every work, every encounter is characterised by an underlying field of thousands of small perceptions, of intensities, desires, dreams, hallucinations, projections. Things are never unified in an absolutely transparent representation. The small perceptions are the mobile elements of a problematic energy. Every work, every creation, every object is inspired and mobilised by the obscure and non-representative forces of a virtual memory. This motivates and orients thinking and ensures the communication between different points of view.

Deleuze thinks through the consequences of Bergson's notion of the virtual in a more radical way. For Deleuze—contrary to Bergson[97]—there is a possibility to have direct access to the virtual by means of the involuntary memory of Marcel Proust and by means of what he calls the *time-image*. In Proust's involuntary memory, the virtual past surges up as it is in itself, as it has never been remembered. It surges up in spite of remembering, in the oblivion itself. Proust's hero has an involuntary memory of the village (Combray) where he spent his childhood holidays in which "Combray rises up in a form that is absolutely new. Combray does not rise up as it was once present; Combray rises up as past, but this past is no longer relative to the

---

[97] For Bergson, pure memory is always involved in a process of materialisation. Direct access to the virtual is impossible.

present in relation to which it is now past. [...] Combray appears as it could not be experienced" (Deleuze 1964, 61). The involuntary memory comes *intact* to us, but this does not mean it is *identical* to the experience we once had. It reveals an experience that has never been present. Proust says:

> And these streets of Combray stretch their existence in such a far part of my memory and they are so completely different in colour than the world is for me, that all of them, to say the truth, the church that dominated the square included, look more unreal then the projected images of the magic lantern; at some moments, it seems to me that the possibility to cross again the street Saint Hilaire or to rent a room in the street Oiseau ... would be a more miraculous and supernatural contact with another world than a personal introduction to Golo or a conversation with Genoveva of Brabant. (Proust 1913, 10; my translation)

Involuntary memory reveals the existence of a virtual memory that has no relation to the psychological representations of a past moment. It stands for a completely different world, an untouchable, unreachable, virginal memory. Also in *The Time-Image*, Deleuze finds direct access to virtual memory. In this image, of which he finds an example in the Italian neo-realist cinema, the obscure pre-individual field in which the imaginary and the real are intimately interwoven becomes 'visible.' The time-image reveals an anarchic mobilisation of virtual desires, dreams, hallucinations, and projections, in which it is impossible to delineate the real from the imaginary.

In Deleuze's ontology of the virtual, the virtual and the actual both belong to the positive nature of desire. Although this ontology concerns different worlds or zones of being, it rejects every conflict, every contradiction or opposition. Instead of *contradiction*, Deleuze talks about a *disjunction*. He conceives this disjunction as a synthesis in which the disjunctive series or elements are not exterior to each other like in Kant's syllogism about God. For Kant, the disjunctive judgment can only be attributed to God because the necessity of God excludes all contingent propositions. For Deleuze, on the contrary, the disjunctive synthesis is inclusive in the Leibnizian and Nietzschean sense that all the disjunctions are different points of view. Sickness and health are not contradictions that exclude each other, but sickness is a point of view, an exploration of health and *vice versa* (Deleuze 1969, 173). This is also the case for the notions of truth and falsehood:

> The false becomes the mode of exploration of the true, the very space of its essential disguises or its fundamental displacement: the *pseudos* here becomes the pathos of the True. (Deleuze 1968, 107)

For Freud, on the contrary, the double development of two different series (the hegemony of the reality principle and of the pleasure principle) leads to conflict. In *The Id and the Ego*, Freud describes how the self is shattered by the different formations that have resulted from the Id. In the outside world, the self is confronted with the demands of reality, which restrict the claims led by the pleasure principle. In order to live in harmony with reality, the claims of the pleasure principle need to be restrained. The formation of conscience (the super-ego) is thereby crucial. According to Freud's theory of the Oedipus complex, the super-ego consists of an interiorised identification with the father. But when the demands of the reality principle in the order of the super-ego become too severe, this can lead to a turn against the self. The destructive components of the drive become dominant and the consequence is a "rift in the ego which never heals but which increases as time goes on. The two contrary reactions to the conflict persist as the centre-point of a splitting of the ego" (SE 23, 276). This leads to all kinds of pathological syndromes. In melancholy, all libidinal energy is withdrawn from the objects. The energy becomes desexualised and flows back to the ego. In neurosis, the ego tries above all to live in harmony with reality and oppresses the claims of the pleasure principle. In psychosis, the demands of pleasure are fulfilled, but reality is denied. In all these cases, the splitting of the ego is never solved. Even when there is a seeming compromise in favour of one of the drives, then it is still at the cost of sickness: neurosis, psychosis, schizophrenia.

To this conflicting theory of Freud's and the domestication of desire in the Oedipus complex, Deleuze opposes his positive conception of desire, which is engaged with virtual objects that coexist with reality. For Deleuze, this presupposes, like in Bergson's theory, a world with two focuses. With his ontology of the virtual, Deleuze intends to overcome Freud's theory of the Oedipus complex. On the same basis as Freud, namely with the chaotic field of excitations and free floating energy (the Id) as starting point, Deleuze wants to disrupt from within the Freudian assumptions. With this purpose in mind, he tries to connect with the partial objects of Freud and Melanie Klein to put them in a completely different perspective. These partial objects are precisely the virtual recollections that he got from Bergson.

Freud mentions partial objects when the object of love is not the person in totality, but parts of the body or certain objects. He describes these partial objects in the context of the phenomenon of fetishism. In *Fetishism*, Freud explains how a little boy discovers with great fear that his mother has no penis. The child supposes that she used to have a penis but that she has been punished by the father with castration. As a consequence, the child denies the absence of his mother's penis and uses a substitute instead. This substitute is the fetish. It is a part of the body or an object on which the curious gaze of the boy rests, the last before the naked body of the woman brings about the evidence that the woman is not phallic:

> Thus the foot or shoe owes its preference as a fetish—or a part of it—to the circumstance that the inquisitive boy peered at the woman's genitals from below, from her legs up; fur and velvet—as has long been suspected—are a fixation of the sight of the pubic hair, which should have been followed by the longed-for sight of the female member, pieces of underclothing, which are so often chosen as a fetish, crystallize the moment of undressing, the last moment in which the woman could still be regarded as phallic. (SE 21, 155)

These partial objects are invested by the drives without reference to the body as a whole. The body as a whole or the lack of the penis of the mother, however, is not repressed by the child, but *disavowed*. Disavowal is, according to Deleuze and contrary to Freud (he relates disavowal to the withdrawal of memory in traumatic amnesia), "the point of departure of an operation that consists neither in negating nor even destroying, but rather in radically contesting the validity of that which is: it suspends belief in and neutralizes the given in such a way that a new horizon opens up beyond the given and in place of it" (Deleuze 1967, 31).

Melanie Klein has elaborated the idea of partial objects in the phantasmatic world of the child. Very young children have not yet—by the insufficiency of their visual capacities—an image of the mother as a complete person. The child attributes qualities that belong to the mother as a complete person to parts of her body, of which the paradigmatic object is the breast. As the child is overwhelmed with a fundamental anxiety from the lack of nourishment, it projects this anxiety which comes from within to the outside world, and reconstructs the world with all kinds of phantasmatic (partial) objects. As such, the child assumes that there is a 'good breast' (this is the breast that nourishes) and a bad breast (this is the breast which refuses food).

Deleuze is enthusiastic about these partial objects, because he considers them as potential arguments against the domestication of desire in the Oedipus complex. The partial objects can indeed not be integrated in the form of the person. Instead of the delineated subjective poles, the mother, the father and the child, the world becomes a phantasmagoria of partial objects. In *Difference and Repetition*, Deleuze states that "when Melanie Klein shows how many virtual objects the maternal body contains, it must not be thought that it totalises or englobes them, or possesses them, but rather that they are planted in it like trees from another world" (Deleuze 1968, 101). Deleuze accentuates the partial and irreducible character of the partial objects, and denies every totalisation of them into the whole of the maternal body. But, in *Anti-Oedipus*, Deleuze regrets that Melanie Klein has not thought through the potential power of the partial objects for a subversion of the Oedipus-complex. She has "not seen the logic of these objects" (Deleuze & Guattari 1972, 52) because she considered the stage of the partial objects as a pre-Oedipal stage in the evolution of the child. For her, "not only are they [the partial objects] destined to play a role in totalities aimed at integrating the ego, the object, and drives later in life, but they also constitute the original type of object relation between the ego, the mother, and the father. And in the final analysis that is where the crux of the matter lies" (44). For Deleuze, on the contrary, the breast is a partial object that is part of a desiring machine:

> Ever since birth, his [the child's] crib, his mother's breast, her nipple, his bowel movements are desiring-machines connected to parts of his body. It seems to us self-contradictory to maintain, on the one hand, that the child lives among partial objects, and that on the other hand he conceives of these partial objects as being his parents, or even different parts of his parents' bodies. Strictly speaking, it is not true that a baby experiences his mother's breast as a separate part of her body. It exists rather, as a part of a desiring-machine connected to the baby's mouth, and is experienced as an object providing a nonpersonal flow of milk, be it copious or scanty. (47)

Deleuze opposes to the Oedipus-complex a theory of positive productions of desire, which are constituted by a repetition in which there is no reference to the father or the mother. "Reminiscence does not simply refer us back from a present present to former ones, from recent loves to infantile ones, from our lovers to our mothers" (Deleuze 1968, 85), he says. This repetition of desire consists of series of partial objects that have no ultimate term; only the mother has a certain place in this chain. No object has a privileged place in it. All of them are equally 'real.' As a consequence, the phantasmatic productions of the virtual objects no longer appear to conflict with reality. This implies that Deleuze attributes reality to the phantasmatic productions. For Freud, on the contrary, they can only have psychic reality. In 'The Interpretation of Dreams,' he says:

> Whether we are to attribute *reality* to the unconscious wishes, I cannot say. It must be denied, of course, to any transitional or intermediate thoughts. If we look at unconscious wishes reduced to their most fundamental and truest shape, we shall have to conclude, no doubt,

that *psychical* reality is a particular form of existence not to be confused with *material* reality. (SE 5, 620)

This is not the kind of reality that Deleuze, following Bergson and Proust, attributes to the phantasmatic. For them, the virtual productions of desire are real. "Real without being actual, ideal without being abstract" is the formulation of Proust. The unconscious desires must not be repressed; they have to be lived through. This statement of Deleuze's fits into his Nietzschean thought that reality should not be interpreted nor evaluated; it must be created. This claim on creation indeed finds its most obvious expression in art. Here Deleuze is strongly opposed to Freud's presupposition that the artist is someone who has to be considered as a 'lost soul' who is locked up in his fantasy and who finally finds the way back to reality by producing works of art. Freud writes:

> Art brings about a reconciliation between the two principles in a peculiar way. An artist is originally a man who turns away from reality because he cannot come to terms with the renunciation of instinctual satisfaction which it at first demands, and who allows his erotic and ambitious wishes full play in the life of phantasy. He finds the way back to reality, however, from this world of phantasy by making use of special gifts to mould his phantasies into truths of a new kind, which are valued by men as precious reflections of reality. Thus in a certain fashion he actually becomes the hero, the king, the creator, or the favourite he desired to be, without following the long roundabout path of making real alterations in the external world. (SE 12, 224)

For Deleuze, on the contrary, the artist is not someone who needs to find a compromise between his fantasy and reality. According to Deleuze, "the artist is the master of objects, converting them to the regime of desiring-machines, breaking down is part of the very functioning of desiring-machines…" (Deleuze & Guattari 1972, 32). The pop-artist Claes Oldenburg is a good example of such an artistic desiring-machine. He uses rotten, broken, recycled, lost objects or things thrown away. In his *Statement* he says: "I am for the brown sad art of rotting apples […]. I am for the art of things lost or thrown away […] decapitated rabbits, exploded umbrellas […] chairs with their brown bones broken, burning trees […]. I am for the art of slightly rotten funeral flowers" (Oldenburg 1961, 215).

About Freud's position concerning the status of the phantasmatic, however, it must be said that he does not qualify the phantasmatic as something purely illusory. In the originary phantasm, Freud discovers unconscious schemata which transcend the experience of the individual and which are inherited. Their universality is situated in a phylogenetic perspective. The originary phantasm refers to 'real events' in a mythological era. The phenomena which are related to the originary phantasm (originary scene, castration, seduction) all refer to a certain 'origin.' Like the collective myths, they provide a 'solution' for the mystery of existence. They present an "event which stands for the beginning of the history of mankind." But, in spite of this real character of the originary phantasms, Deleuze criticizes the idea of an 'origin.' He wants to think of repetition as a dynamism that is not related to a beginning or an end. He states: "There are no ultimate or original responses or solutions, there are only problem-questions, in the guise of a mask behind every mask and a displacement behind every place" (Deleuze 1968, 107).

This brings him to the development of a third synthesis. The second synthesis, the connection of Eros and Mnemosynè, still suffers from an ambiguity. This ambiguity consists in the fact that the erotic memory can take itself for a final foundation, that it presents itself as an absolute origin. Plato's reminiscence is not far from this idea. It is also this ambiguity still present in the second synthesis that brings Alain Badiou, who has always criticized virtual memory, to his interpretation of Deleuze as a 'platonist of the virtual.' To this virtual memory, Badiou wants to oppose a more fundamental oblivion. He remarks:

> It is essential for me to think of the truth not as a time or as the timeless being of time, but as *interruption*. It seems to me that Deleuze and Hegel state that truth is definitely memory, the incorporation in being of its actualised plenitude that belongs absolutely to the past [...]. But when the 'there is' is pure plurality, when everything is actual, when the One is not, it is not at the side of memory that truth should be searched. Truth on the contrary is forgetful. (Badiou 1997, 96–99; my translation)

But while Badiou considers Deleuze a thinker of memory, he forgets that Deleuze has opened up the foundation of memory towards a third synthesis. In this third synthesis, every foundation becomes groundless. This is a synthesis in which the objects disappear and the subject dissolves in order to establish an ascetic minimalism. With this third synthesis, the recollections, the objects of desire, and every origin and every identity are unmasked as illusions of what Deleuze calls the optical effects of memory. The result is a man without name, "without memory, a great amnesiac [...] and without love" (Deleuze 1968, 111).

4. The third synthesis

With the third synthesis, Deleuze constitutes the conditions for a complete liberation of desire. Desire is then no longer restricted by the form of the subject or the object. The self becomes dissolved. The crucial moment in this dissolution is what Freud called a desexualisation. According to Freud, desexualisation is the consequence of the conflict between the pleasure principle and the demands of reality. The ego wants to heal the fracture between the two series by interiorising them both, but it is not capable of doing this because of its fundamental passivity. As a consequence, the libidinal energy flows back to the self and undergoes a desexualisation. In *The Ego and the Id,* Freud mentions a neutral, mobile, and transformable energy:

> We have reckoned as though there existed in the mind—whether in the ego or in the id—a displaceable energy, which, neutral in itself, can be added to a qualitatively differentiated erotic or destructive impulse, and augment its total cathexis. Without assuming the existence of a displaceable energy of this kind we can make no headway. (SE 19, 44)

Deleuze remarks that Freud needs desexualisation for the constitution of the narcissistic self and the formation of the super-ego. The desexualised energy can be used for varying processes; "it is the equivalent of a process of *idealization*, which can perhaps constitute the power of the imagination in the ego," or "the equivalent of *identification*" (Deleuze 1967, 116).

When the desexualised energy is used for processes of sublimation, this leads to a pleasure of a higher order. When the pleasure principle transgresses itself towards the higher works of culture, desexualisation is not in conflict with or in opposition to the pleasure principle. But, next to sublimation, Freud also mentions the possibility for this neutralised energy to be put at the service of the destructive drives or death drives, which are opposed to the pleasure principle. For Freud, this leads to pathology. For Deleuze, on the contrary, there is a third synthesis in which the conflict is resolved. Although he follows Freud in his idea of desexualised energy in close relation to the death drives, he understands this as a positive, joyful event. The desexualised energy stands for a radical movement of deterritorialisation. Next to the processes of sublimation or pathology, Deleuze states that there is a third possibility in which the desexualised energy is 'at work,' namely *perversion*:

> And is not this the very alternative indicated by Freud under the name of perversion? It is remarkable that the process of *desexualisation* is even more pronounced than in neurosis and sublimation; it operates with

extraordinary coldness; but it is accompanied by a *resexualization* which does not in any way cancel out the desexualisation, since it operates in a new dimension which is equally remote from functional disturbances and from sublimations. (Deleuze 1967, 117)

This implies a conception of perversion different from the traditional conception of it. Traditionally perversion is "a deviation from the 'normal' sexual act when this is defined as coitus with a person of the opposite sex directed towards the achievement of orgasm by means of genital penetration" (Laplanche & Pontalis 1967, 306). According to this definition, other sexual objects or purposes are perverted. For Deleuze, however, perversion is not a deviation from objects or purposes, but an intrinsic transformation of energy. It becomes neutralised by a movement of deterritorialisation in order to find a free and endless circulation. Desire becomes endless by a suspense instead of a satisfaction. This is the case in masochism. Deleuze states that the objective of masochism is not pain or humiliation. These only constitute the price the masochist pays to postpone satisfaction in favour of an unlimited energy that circulates on an endless plane of immanence. The pain and the torture are means to keep every sensuality (if it be erotic or sadistic sensuality) at a distance so that desire becomes a *super-sensual* pleasure that operates in a new order, in which the father is denied and the mother becomes the instance of the law. As the fetishist who denies the lack of the penis of the woman and whose gaze installs a suspense, the masochist denies the phallic order and aims at a second birth of the new man, a parthenogenesis coming only from the mother. With masochism, Deleuze can break the phallic order of the symbolic that is oriented towards 'the name of the father.'

In relation to masochism and this different conception of perversion, Deleuze also presents a different conception of the death drive. Whereas Freud considers masochism as the reverse of sadism and understands both perversions as dynamics which obey the death drive, in which masochism is aggression turned against the self, Deleuze does not understand the death drive as an aggressive and destructive energy which exists in conflict with life. To him, the death drive is not itself related to the empirical contents of life. It is a transcendental principle which is the condition of empirical pleasure. It is a silent principle that is not 'active' in life. The desexualisation of energy is not at the service of the death drive—or 'death instinct,' which he prefers (Deleuze 1967, 30). The death instinct is itself desexualised energy. As such, it does not enter into the circle of Eros-Mnemosynè, but constitutes it. This explains why Deleuze has never understood the 'Jenseits' in *Jenseits des Lustprinzips* as the 'beyond' which conflicts with life. He has always understood it as the condition of the pleasure principle. In his *Coldness and Cruelty*, Deleuze says:

> We must conclude that the pleasure principle, though it may rule over all, does not have the final or highest authority over all. There are no exceptions to the principle but there is a residue that is irreducible to it; nothing contradicts the principle, but there remains something which falls outside it and is not homogeneous with it—something, in short, *beyond* ... (Deleuze 1967, 112)

This 'beyond' in its transcendental meaning constitutes an autonomous synthesis of time: a third synthesis. It is not complementary or antagonistic to the second synthesis. The death instinct cuts all bonds with the memories, the virtual objects, and the infantile phantasms. The energy is not an energy of conflict; it is the questioning energy of the problematic:

> For death cannot be reduced to negation, neither to the negative of opposition nor to the negative of limitation. It is neither the limitation imposed by matter upon mortal life, nor the opposition between matter and immortal life, which furnishes death with its prototype. Death is rather, the last form of the problematic, the source of problems and questions, the sign of their persistence over and above every response. (Deleuze 1968, 112)

With the death instinct, Deleuze realises his project of the dissolution of the self. Death has, for him, following Maurice Blanchot, two aspects. Firstly, it is the disappearance of the person, the reduction to zero of the difference which stands for a distinct person. This reduction is objectively represented as a return to inanimate matter. But, secondly, death is a state of free differences that are no longer subordinated to the form of the ego, the subject, or the object. Deleuze reproaches Freud for only considering the first aspect of death, the materialistic death that consists of a return to inanimate matter. To this second aspect of death, he relates the Leibnizian notion of small perceptions. Instead of the big, conflicting representations and principles of Freud, death opens up to multiplicities of small elements that form continuous series.

Blanchot conceives of this second aspect as a radical 'outside' [*dehors*]. Death is that 'outside' that renders the person impersonal. It stands for that which the person cannot appropriate but which is, at the same time, the most intimate to him:

> My death must become always more inward. It must be like my invisible form, my gesture, the silence of my most hidden secret. There is something I must do to accomplish it, indeed, everything remains for me to do: it must be my work. But this work is beyond me, it is that part of me upon which I shed no light, which I do not attain and of which I am not master. (Blanchot 1955, 126)

For Deleuze, this problematic force of death should be affirmed and lived through even when it renders us impersonal. Death is a work to be done; it is an inspiration, but it is a work or an inspiration that can never be realised, although it must be accomplished. It is a force that is at work in life in an immanent way. As such, death is the model of the future, of the radically new, the unexpected, the undetermined, which establishes a highly paradoxical relation: a non-relation. In this (non-)relation, the objects are lost and the self is dissolved, like the artist who is always exposed to the outside of his art. Every work of art questions everything. According to Blanchot, the act of creation implies that the artist disavows that there is already a work of art, that there is already a world. The artist does not know what art is, he does not know that he is an artist at all, he does not know what inspiration is, and, though he is dependent upon it, he has to invent his own objectives and even his own obstacles. Death is the model of this radical outside, in respect to which man becomes impersonal.

This is precisely the third synthesis of time. As (non-)relation, it is the model of the future. As such, time becomes a static synthesis. The conflicts of the empirical contents of life have disappeared and we enter the domain of its transcendental conditions. This is a repetition which is not empirically given; it is a repetition which does not repeat itself, but which gives repetition. With the characterisation of time as a static synthesis, Deleuze means that time becomes a pure and formal order. In this respect, he returns to Kant and his idea of time as an 'empty form.' But instead of relating this empty form of time to the concepts of the understanding, Deleuze conceives of this empty form as an autonomous repetition which has lost its objects and which gains an endless force of repetition. When time becomes a static synthesis, it does not mean that no change is possible anymore; it means that time is no longer subordinated to movement or change, and that time becomes its own measure. It is the succession of a succession.

Deleuze refers to Hamlet: "Time is out of joint." Time stops being cardinal and becomes ordinal. The 'joint' can be understood in terms of cardinality. In the technical speech of furniture making, the 'cardinal' stands for the hinge around which a door opens and closes. The cardinal is the joint that determines the movement. When Deleuze says, with Hamlet, that time is out of joint, he means that time is no longer subordinated to such hinges. Time becomes pure order, pure 'in between': "Time itself unfolds [...] instead of things unfolding within it" (Deleuze 1968, 88). The result is that time becomes independent of God, men, and nature. Time becomes an autonomous order, a rhythm, a repetition and return, or, as Nietzsche puts it, *an eternal return*. The eternal return installs, as Klossowski points out, "a coherence that is so perfect, it excludes my own coherence" (Klossowski 1967, 234). In the eternal return, everything comes back, not only the interesting, the joyful, or the good moments, but life in its smallest and most meaningless details. No ground of expectation or anticipation by means of acquired identifications or convictions can discipline the chaotic disjunctions of this excessive, problematic energy. The excessive contains all of the possible, in the figure of the empty form of time. It belongs to a secret coherence that destroys the coherence of God, men, and nature. What is left is the groundless play of coincidence.

5. Affirmation and creation

The dissolution of the self implies a highly paradoxical experience. This affirmation is no longer the affirmation of a subject. It is an affirmation that happens in spite of the subject. This is precisely the case with the *duende*. In the *duende*, an impersonal energy flows through the person. He participates in a coherence which excludes his own coherence. Moreover, the *duende* is not only about graceful joy, it implies also an intimate interlace with pain and death in which death is not denied or destroyed, but becomes elevated to the highest impersonal affirmation. The highest intensive emotional state that accompanies it tends to its utter paradoxical figure: insensitivity. García Lorca refers to the singer El Lebrijano, who once said, "On days when I sing with *duende*, no one can touch me" (García Lorca 1933, 3).

In the *duende*, an immanent force is revealed that does not proceed from any transcendent instance. Its affirmation surges up from the earth or the blood; it surges up from the soles of the feet. It comes from the most ancient cultures but, at the same time, the *duende* is not determined or conserved by the ideas of the tradition: it is, like the waves of the sea—and paradoxically enough—unrepeatable in its very repetition. As such, it produces a singular force that is liberated from the subject, the object, and tradition. The dissolved self floats on an activity that is no longer limited. It regains the nature of a force that is no longer oriented against something, but a force that works by itself. The combination of the dissolution of the self and its affirmation requires a repetition that becomes automatic. This is a repetition in which there are no reactive forces and in which everything happens as the innocence of becoming, or, as Heraclitus said, as the innocence of a child's game, insofar as it is a game that is not played to win, but a game that is played only for the sake of playing.

Pablo Picasso—who considered himself the indestructible Andalusian hero who was in the grip of the *duende*—once said that, when he was a child, he could already paint with the precision of Velasquez, and that, after having gone through academic training, at the age of an adult, he was finally capable of painting like a child. This reminds us of the three metamorphoses about which Nietzsche spoke in his *Zarathustra*: The camel becomes a lion and the lion becomes a child. The camel is prepared to offer himself to the world, and carries the burdens of the world. The lion, on the contrary, stands up for himself and fights for his own ideals. Finally, the child stands for the nature of an activity that does not require the conscious and reflected effort of a rational or moral subject. The child is innocence and forgetting, through which it is capable of creating the radically new and re-inventing itself in a continuous, creative repetition: "The child is innocence and forgetting, a new beginning, a game, a wheel rolling out of itself, a first movement, a sacred yes-saying" (Nietzsche 1883–1885, 17). This appears to be the case for Picasso. He created a huge number of styles and aspects in painting which he afterwards destroyed to create new ones. This destruction is no negative reaction or defence. It is more a sort of leaving behind, of forgetting the old to create the new. It has more to do with a passivity in which something happens in spite of the person, than with the activity of a conscious subject. This means that the 'child' does not stand for a process of infantilism, nor regression to a primitive stage but, on the contrary, for the highest forms of creativity as the result of a fundamental passivity which consists in 'becoming less' to be 'more': "To become is to become more and more restrained, more and more deserted and for that reason populated [...] it is also the opposite of regression, returning to a childhood or to a primitive world" (Deleuze & Parnet 1977, 22).

Inspired by Nietzsche, Picasso always searched for the dark forces of the Dionysian, the ecstatic, and the unstable. That this extreme desire for intensity can easily be confused with the fragmentation and destruction in (a pathological conception of) schizophrenia is shown in the writings of Carl Jung. On November 13, 1932, Jung wrote in the *Neue Züricher Zeitung* that Picasso had much in common with the schizophrenic who "presented in his work the always returning characteristic theme of the descent into hell, into the unconscious, and the leaving behind of the outside world." But if Picasso suffered from schizophrenia, the least that could be said is that there is a big difference between him and the schizophrenic patient who is confined to the sickbed and who is unable to do any creative activity whatsoever. In *Anti-Oedipus*, Deleuze develops, with Félix Guattari, an affirmative conception of schizophrenia as the most extreme figure of a dissolution of the self, in which the creative forces of the dissolution of libidinal energy are accentuated. This problematic conception of schizophrenia raises a lot of questions, but, concerning Picasso, we can say that there was indeed a creative and affirmative force at work through him. And, concerning Nietzsche, Martial Guéroult remarks:

> We have to think about the final destination of the philosophy of Nietzsche: this philosophy with all its destructive forces, tends completely, until the last moment, to an ideal of affirmation, of joy, almost of beatitude. (Guéroult 1967, 10)

With this paradox of an impersonal affirmation, Deleuze comes close to the Nietzschean and Spinozist idea of 'amor fati.' This is an affirmation of a necessary order in which one cannot choose one's fate. It is the affirmation of a 'pure event' that is characterised by a problematic energy which makes possible an affirmation of all its disjunctive terms. This is precisely the ontological expression of Deleuze's three syntheses. With the event, Deleuze develops an ontology of pure immanence. He relies on John Duns Scotus to think a neutralisation of Being, so that Being becomes the univocal name for the plurality of things. Like the neutralisation of the libidinal energy in the process of desexualisation, Being is released from the categories that form the hierarchy of Being in the theory of analogy. As such, it becomes a neutral concept that can express all differences in their most subtle distinctions.

With Spinoza, Deleuze wants to transform Duns Scotus' neutralised concept into an affirmative concept of expression. Univocal being expresses itself in all things, and all things are the expression of being. Philosophy becomes an endless plane of immanence in which everything is interwoven with everything. Like the reterritorialisations of desire (in which desire produces itself in the same way—without any conflicts—in all of the different cases), being is affirmed in all its expressions. This thinking of immanence demands an ascetic exercise to leave behind all existing symbolic categories, all acquired knowledge, convictions, and expectations to open oneself to the multiple reterritorialisations of desire, the expressions of univocal being, and the production of differences.

This brings us back to the image of the nomad. The nomad is the person who leaves all redundancies behind, who can detach from his roots and begin over and over again as a continual re-beginning, which has nothing to do with a transcendent instance. The nomad is the one who is always close to the elemental forces of the earth. This is also the case with the *duende*, which has always been described in chthonic terms. García Lorca writes: "This mysterious force, which everyone feels and no philosopher has explained, is, in sum, the spirit of the earth ..." (García Lorca 1933, 3). The *duende* is in the earth, in the veins, in the fibres of the body, in the blood. No lack or negativity, no distant contemplation of a higher being, no resignation, no mysticism can reach it. The *duende* is a force of the earth, although it can never be localised somewhere on the earth. Strictly speaking, it can never be searched for somewhere; it can only be found. It occurs. Or, as García Lorca writes:

The *duende* ... where is the *duende*? Through the empty archway a wind of the spirit enters, blowing insistently over the heads of the dead, in search of new landscapes and unknown accents: a wind with the odour of a child's saliva, crushed grass, and medusa's veil, announcing the endless baptism of freshly created things. (García Lorca 1933,10)

Bibliography

Badiou, A. 1997. *Deleuze: 'La clamour de l'être.'* Paris: Hachette, 1997.
Bergson, H. 1919. *Mind-Energy: Lectures and Essays*. Translated by W. Carr. London: Macmillan, 1920.
———. 1939. *Matter and Memory*. Translated by N. M. Paul. Mineola, NY: Dover, 2004.
Blanchot, M. 1955. *The Space of Literature*. Translated and with an introduction by A. Smock. Lincoln: University of Nebraska press, 1982.
Deleuze, G. 1953. *Empiricism and Subjectivity: An Essay on Hume's Theory of Human Nature*. Translated and with an introduction by C. V. Boundas. New York: Columbia University Press, 1991.
———. 1964. *Proust and Signs*. Translated by R. Howard. Minneapolis: University of Minnesota Press, 2000.
———. 1967. 'Coldness and cruelty.' In *Masochism*. Translated by J. McNeil. New York: Zone Books, 1989, pp. 8-138
———. 1968. *Difference and Repetition*. Translated by P. Patton. London: Athlone, 1994.

———. 1969. *The Logic of Sense*. Translated by M. Lester and C. Stivale. Edited by C. V. Boundas. London: Athlone, 1990.

———. 1985. *Cinema 2: The Time-image*. Translated by H. Tomlinson. London: Athlone, 1989.

Deleuze, G., and F. Guattari. 1972. *Anti-Oedipus: Capitalism and Schizophrenia*. Translated by R. Hurley, M. Seem, and H. R. Lane. Minneapolis: University of Minnesota Press, 1983.

Deleuze, G., and C. Parnet. 1977. *Dialogues*. Translated by H. Tomlinson and B. Habberjam. London: Continuum, 2002.

Freud, S. 1911. 'Formulations of Two Principles of Mental Functioning.' SE 12.

———. 1920. 'Beyond the Pleasure Principle.' SE 18.

———. 1923. 'The Ego and the Id.' SE 19.

———. 1927. 'Fetishism.' SE 21.

———. 1930 [1899]. 'The Interpretation of Dreams.' SE 5.

———. 1940 [1938]. 'Splitting of the Ego in the Process of Defence.' SE 23.

García Lorca, Federico. 1933. 'Theory and Play of the *Duende*.' Translated by A. S. Kline. http://www.tonykline.co.uk/PITBR/Spanish/LorcaDuende.htm. 2004.

Guéroult, M. 1967. 'Introduction.' In *Nietzsche—Cahiers de Royaumont*. Paris: Les Éditions de Minuit, 1967.

Kant, I. 1781. *Critique of Pure Reason*. Translated by P. Guyer. Cambridge: Cambridge University Press, 1998.

Klossowski, P. 1967. 'Oubli et anamnèse dans l'expérience vécue de l'éternel retour du même.' In *Nietzsche—Cahiers de Royaumont*. Paris: Les Éditions de Minuit, 1967, pp. 228-234.

Laplanche, J., and J.-B. Pontalis. 1967. *The Language of Psycho-analysis*. Translated by D. Nicholson-Smith. London: Karnac, 1973.

Leibniz, G. W. 1704. *New Essays on Human Understanding*. Edited and translated by P. Remnant and J. Bennett. Cambridge: Cambridge University Press, 1981.

Maïmon, S. 1790. *Versuch über die Transzendentalphilosophie*. Hamburg: Meiner, 2004.

Nietzsche, F. 1883–1885. *Thus Spoke Zarathustra: A Book for All and None*. Edited by A. del Caro and R. B. Pippin. Translated by A. del Caro. Cambridge: Cambridge University Press, 2006.

Oldenburg, C. 1961. 'Statement.' In *Pop Art, A Critical History*. Edited by S. H. Madoff. Berkeley: University of California Press, 1997, pp. 213-215.

Proust, M. 1913. *Du Côté de chez Swann—À la recherche du temps perdu 1*. Paris: Gallimard, 1987.

Stassinopoulos Huffington, A. 1988. *Picasso, Creator and Destroyer*. New York: Simon and Schuster, 1988.

Epilogue

Leen De Bolle

Nowadays, it is interesting to see how Deleuze has populated the landscape of philosophy with a huge number of new concepts. Not only did he inject existing concepts with new meanings (e.g. desire, love, the unconscious, repetition, perversion, masochism, partial objects, etc.), he also created many concepts all his own (e.g. rhizome, de- and reterritorialisations, ritornel, desiring machines, lines of flight, etc.). As the contributions in this volume show, Deleuze's wide range of interests, and the many questions he raised, have elicited a large variety of discussions. The literature on Deleuze has figured in many different domains, of which psychoanalysis is only one of many. The great variety of literature produced in response to Deleuze is a direct consequence of his 'philosophy of difference,' with its neologisms and its creative approach to concepts. Deleuze's philosophy of becoming, of the dynamic coincidence with the openness of an ever-changing life, the fluidly mouldable streams of energy always ready to transform, to disguise, or to displace themselves, has shattered all fixed and stable concepts. Concepts need to be 'dramatized.' They must be put on stage; they must be played.

Contrary to appearances, however, these new meanings of existing concepts, along with the newly created concepts, are the elements of a consistent system. In spite of the chaotic disorganization, the unpredictable events, the multiplicities, the pluralist patchwork, the fragmentary and utterly dense style of writing, Deleuze is, as he declares himself in a letter to Jean-Clet Martin, a 'systematic' thinker. Unlike the mathematical system of Descartes or the dialectical system of Hegel, however, Deleuze's 'system' is not characterised by a vertical structure or a constructivist logic, but rather by a horizontal orientation in which everything is intertwined with everything else. Consequently, we might say the same thing about Deleuze's philosophy as he said about Spinoza's system—that it is the "most absolute totality" and, nevertheless, "we have the feeling that we will never manage to grasp it in its entirety. We fail to grasp the totality. We are not fast enough to keep everything together."[98] Deleuze adds to this statement that Spinoza is "of all philosophers, the one who disposes of the most systematic conceptual apparatus, and nevertheless, we as readers, have always the impression that

---

[98] G. Deleuze, Spinoza lesson at Vincennes 25/11/1980. www.webdeleuze.com, 5.

we miss the totality of it and that we are always affected by one or another fragment." This statement can be linked with what Klossowski said about Nietzsche's concept of the eternal return, that the concept is so perfectly coherent, that it excludes my own coherence.[99] If such a philosophical system can be interpreted as a perfectly coherent totality that we can nevertheless never completely grasp, then this philosophy is able to produce an endless variety of discussions.

Yet, at the same time, one could wonder why the literature on Deleuze was so long in coming. Even though Deleuze had long been present in French philosophy, it is only in the past ten years that the production of secondary literature on the international scene has intensified. Deleuze can certainly be considered one of the great contemporary French philosophers but, unlike his contemporaries (e.g. Foucault, Derrida, Sartre, Lacan, Merleau-Ponty, Lyotard, etc.), for a long time he was less commonly known abroad. Possibly this is also owing to the fact that his philosophical system is so difficult to grasp. But, as time has unmistakably shown, it is worthwhile to explore his difficult oeuvre, since it has come to be of major importance in contemporary philosophy and of great influence in the way we conceptualise nowadays in art and literature, in psychoanalysis, and in many other domains.

This is the challenge to us today: to think and rethink Deleuze's notions in a context that keeps changing, in discussion with psychoanalysis, with art and literature, with political, ethical, or other questions, to find new entrances or exits in the rhizomatic texture of life, to create new lines of flight.

---

[99] Cfr. P. Klossowski, "Oubli et anamnèse dans l'expérience vécue de l'éternel retour du même". In *Nietzsche*, Cahiers de Royaumont, Paris, Les Éditions de Minuit, 1967, pp. 228, 234.

List of Contributors

Tomas Geyskens is doctor in philosophy, master in sexology, and a practising psychoanalyst. He works in private practice in Leuven, Belgium, and in Zonnelied, Roosdaal, Belgium. In collaboration with Philippe Van Haute, he published *Confusion of tongues* (Other Press 2004) and *From death instinct to attachment theory* (Other Press 2007).

Lyat Friedman teaches at the Philosophy Department and the Gender Studies Program at Bar Ilan University in Israel. She is the author of the forthcoming text: *In the Footsteps of Psychoanalysis* (Bar Ilan University Press, 2010).

Christian Kerslake is a Lecturer in Modern European Philosophy at the Centre for Research in Modern European Philosophy, Middlesex University, London. He is the author of *Deleuze and the Unconscious* (Continuum, 2007) and *Immanence and the Vertigo of Philosophy: From Kant to Deleuze* (Edinburgh, 2009), and the co-editor of *Origins and Ends of the Mind* (Leuven University Press, 2007).

Peter Hallward teaches at the Centre for Research in Modern European Philosophy at Middlesex University, and is the author of *Damming the Flood: Haiti and the Politics of Containment* (2007), *Out of this World: Deleuze and the Philosophy of Creation* (2006), *Badiou: A Subject to Truth* (2003), and *Absolutely Postcolonial* (2001).

Éric Alliez, is Professor of Contemporary French Philosophy at the Centre for Research in Modern European Philosophy (Middlesex University, London). His works include: *Les Temps capitaux* (preface by G. Deleuze), T.I, *Récits de la conquête du temps* (Paris: Cerf, 1991 [English Transl. : *Capital Times*, Minneapolis: U. of Minnesota, 1997] - T. II, *La Capitale du temps*, Vol. 1 : *L'Etat des choses* (Paris: Cerf, 1999); *La Signature du monde, ou Qu'est-ce que la philosophie de Deleuze et Guattari ?* (Paris: Cerf, 1993) [English Transl. with two new appendixes: *The Signature of the World. Or What is the Philosophy of Deleuze and Guattari?*, London: Continuum, 2005] ; *De l'impossibilité de la phénoménologie. Sur la philosophie française contemporaine* (Paris: Vrin, 1995);

Deleuze Philosophie Virtuelle (Paris: Synthélabo, 1996) ; *Gilles Deleuze. Une Vie philosophique* (editor) (Paris: Synthélabo, 1998).Most recent books : *La Pensée-Matisse* (with J.-Cl. Bonne) (Paris : Le Passage, 2005) ; *L'Œil-Cerveau. Nouvelles Histoires de la peinture moderne* (in collaboration with Jean-Clet Martin) (Paris: Vrin, 2007). He is currently working on *Défaire l'Image*, the last volume of his 'aesthetic' research programme.

Lightning Source UK Ltd.
Milton Keynes UK
UKHW010129121022
410341UK00001B/23